Trevor Millum

SON
of the SECRET GARDENER

The story of the gardening father and son behind
the famous novel by the Secret Gardener's grandson

Quadrant Books

First published in 2021 by Quadrant Books
A member of the Memoirs Group
Suite 2, Top Floor, 7 Dyer Street, Cirencester, Gloucestershire, GL7 2PF

A catalogue record for this book is available from the British Library

Son of the Secret Gardener

Paperback ISBN 978-1-86151-993-1

Typeset by Ray Lipscombe Design, Cirencester
Printed and bound in Great Britain

Son of the Secret Gardener

Trevor Millum

Illustrations by Twink Addison

The Son of the Secret Gardener

This story has its roots in the life of George Owen Millum, who at the turn of the 19th century was the head gardener at Maytham Hall in Kent, the home of Frances Hodgson Burnett, long celebrated for her timeless classic *The Secret Garden*. The garden in the story was based upon that at Maytham Hall, and George Millum was the model for Ben Weatherstaff, Frances Hodgson Burnett's fictional gardener. George's son, George Charles Millum, who like his father was born in the gardener's cottage at Maytham, also grew up to be a country house gardener – hence the title of this book, written and compiled by his own son with detailed extracts from his diaries.

My father worked with a fork and spade

My father worked with a fork and spade
His hands rough with the pulling of weeds
And the management of handle and blade.
The shed bench littered with packets of seeds.

An expert. He would set the seedlings
In neat rows labelled with Latin names:
Rows made straight with sticks and string.
In the greenhouse, in the cold frame,

His eye narrowed and angled on aphid
Or wasp. He'd use knife, fingers or
Pungent poisonous fumes to rid
The greenhouse of pests. I saw

A navy-blue apron with pockets for plants,
Secateurs, clasp knife, bits of bass
To tie up the dahlias, tomatoes, chrysanths;
I'd 'help' if I could with each task.

'Don't be a gardener, son,' he'd say.
It wasn't the work, but the pay.
He was glad when books took me away
And gave me things he'd never had.

But gardening was in the blood
And though books took me far and wide
I've come back to dig and sow
And wish that he could see our garden now.

FOR
DANIEL, JOSEPH
AND DUNCAN

CONTENTS

Introduction

A LIFE IN
GARDENING

This story of gardeners' lives is not written from the point of view of the famous or wealthy, nor is it the reflections of a life in gardening written in tranquil retirement. It is the inside story of those who maintained the grand gardens of the well-to-do in the first half of the twentieth century. It shows how the owners of the gardens of the 'big house' relied on the knowledge and hard work of low-paid servants to keep them supplied with fruit, vegetables and flowers. In addition, they had to keep the paths swept, the lawns immaculate and the tennis courts rolled.

Though not as arduous as the work of the farm labourer, the working days of the gardener involved repetitive, back-aching work in all weathers. The job also required a huge amount of knowledge, gained through unofficial apprenticeships and experience; knowledge of the common and Latin names of plants, of pesticides and fertilizers, of mowers and boilers.

The story begins with a famous name, Frances Hodgson Burnett, and her most famous book, *The Secret Garden*. She lived at Maytham

A Life in Gardening

Hall in Kent, where she gained the inspiration for the book. The head gardener there was my grandfather, George Owen Millum, a model for Ben Weatherstaff in the book. My father, George Charles Millum (who was born in the gardener's cottage at Maytham) also grew up to be a gardener and he was, therefore, the Son of The Secret Gardener.

My father kept meticulous diaries of his work. I have transcribed two of those diaries, for 1935 and 1949, in this book. They offer a unique insight into the day-to-day jobs he and others like him carried out year after year.

The days of the great house and its gardens are over. There are stately homes and large gardens, of course, but they are maintained in different ways and with a very different ethos. Perhaps today's gardeners are keeping similar records on their tablets or phones, but I wonder if they will survive as well as these pencilled entries in these battered journals?

The American writer and the
English garden

Frances Hodgson Burnett

It was a while before I put two and two together. Maytham Hall, the home of Frances Hodgson Burnett from the late 1890s to 1909, was often mentioned by older members of the family, as was the writer herself. "Yes, she gave a pram as a gift when George was born," said Auntie Rachel. It went over my head at the time. Later, I read *The Secret Garden* and even later, as I was sorting through family documents, I realised that my grandfather was the gardener at Maytham Hall. He *was* the Secret Gardener!

It was not until she had returned to America that Frances completed, in 1909, her famous children's novel *The Secret Garden*, published in 1911. The story, with its descriptions of the walled garden, the robin and the irascible gardener was entirely inspired

George Owen Millum (right)

by Maytham Hall, though moved to the more romantic Yorkshire wilds, a place for which there is no evidence of her ever visiting.

My grandfather, George Owen Millum, was the Head Gardener during Frances Hodgson Burnett's tenancy at Maytham. Although only 30 in 1909, we know he could be an obstinate and sometimes difficult fellow. Disguised by the novelist's pen, he is the model for Hodgson Burnett's gruff gardener, made older, given a Yorkshire accent and renamed Ben Weatherstaff – much more appropriate than George Millum! 'He had a surly old face, and did not seem at all pleased to see her – but then she was displeased with his garden and wore her "quite contrary" expression, and certainly did not seem at all pleased to see him.'

So says Mary, upon whom the novel centres. Brought up in India, Mary has been orphaned and is sent to England to live with a widowed uncle at his Yorkshire estate. She hears of the late Mrs. Craven's walled garden, which was locked by the uncle on his wife's death. Mary is determined to find it and in doing so encounters the surly gardener Ben Weatherstaff, whom she gradually befriends. One day, following a friendly robin, Mary discovers an old key which allows her to enter the secret garden. She finds it overgrown, but begins clearing and weeding it.

One day she meets Dickon, the maid's brother and a lover of nature, who helps her in the garden. Later, Mary hears the cries of her supposedly sick and crippled 10-year-old cousin, Colin, who has been confined to the house. He and Mary become friends, and she discovers that he does not have a spinal deformation, as he has believed. Dickon and Mary take Colin to see the garden, and there he discovers that he is able to stand. The three children explore the garden together and plant seeds to revitalize it, and through their friendship and interactions with nature they grow healthier and happier.

The story was first published in serial form in ten episodes and then in book form in 1911. It was not initially as popular as other books by Burnett such as *Little Lord Fauntleroy,* but over the years it has become one of our best loved children's books, with many film and TV adaptations.

There are two major biographies of Hodgson Burnett: *Beyond the Secret Garden* by Ann Thwaite (Duckworth 2020), an updated version of her 1974 biography *Waiting for the Party*, and *Frances Hodgson Burnett* by Gretchen Gerzina (Chatto & Windus 2004). Both books mention the Millums. In 1973, Ann Thwaite interviewed George Millum's cousin, Harry. The following is from *Beyond the Secret Garden*: *'The other person who remembered Frances was Harry Millum. His father worked at the Hall for many years as a gardener and Harry went there as a stable lad in 1898, just at the time Frances took over the house. He was twelve and earned half a crown a week.'* (FHB would often write in the Rose Garden.)

'The gardeners knew not to disturb her. 'It was as if she had something inside her she just had to get out,' Harry Millum said, looking back seventy years. Harry Millum does not seem to think the gardeners at Maytham appreciated Frances' actual gardening, but her letters record her transplanting seedlings and pruning.'

She had returned to Maytham for only six weeks after her trip to Montreux, and when she sailed for America late in March, the Maytham servants were bereft and pooled together to buy her a gift. 'We one & all are taking the liberty to wish you health wealth and *every* happiness and a very pleasant voyage,' they wrote in a note of farewell. 'We all hope to have the Pleasure of Serving you again at dear Old Maytham.' It was signed by 'your Faithfull Servants,' George Millum, Harry Millum, Emily Coombers, David Piper, Emily Judge, Mary Barrett, Herbert Barrett and Tom Barrett. The Maytham servants hoped, like Frances, that she would return to live in the Hall." (page 253)

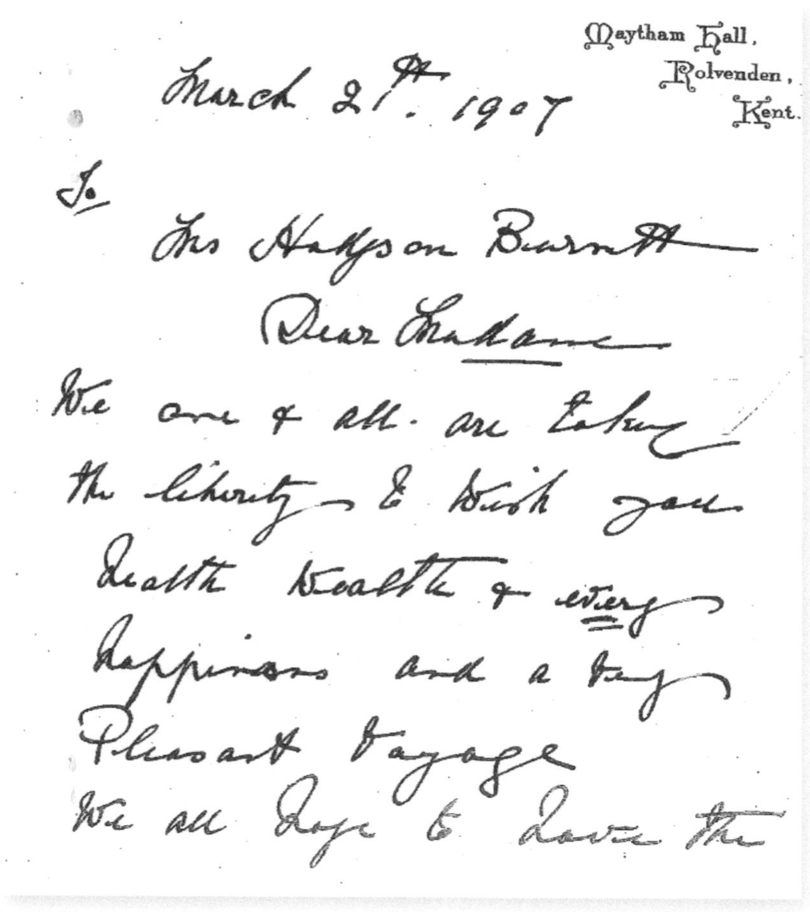

Maytham Hall.
Rolvenden,
Kent.

March 21. 1907

To

Mrs Hodgson Burnett

Dear Madame

We one & all. are taking the liberty & wish you health wealth & every happiness and a very Pleasant Voyage

We all hope to have the

Ref. footnote 9 to FHB from the Maytham servants, 21 March 1907, Special Collections, Boston University Library, no. 1444, box 1, folder 1.

She did not, in fact return to dear Old Maytham, which may have led indirectly to my grandfather leaving service there – see below.

There is a tablet to Frances Hodgson Burnett's memory in the church of St Mary the Virgin Rolvenden, where all the Millums born here were baptised and where a number were married and buried.

Maytham Hall

· Feb 28 1907	1907 May. 5. No. 1750	George Charles	George Owen × alice Jane	Millum.	Maytham Hall Lodge.	Gardener.	J.B.Drabble

My father, George *Charles* Millum, was born in the gardener's cottage attached to Maytham Hall, Rolvenden, in 1907. That building is still there, largely unchanged. I visited it in 1999 and spoke to the current resident and to the gardener in the walled garden. She (a sign of how some things had changed over time) showed us around the walled garden and explained how little of the extensive Edwardian gardens remained. The accommodation for Head

Head Gardener's Cottage, where both my father and grandfather were born

Gardeners could be, as you can see, quite substantial. Their job would be administrative as well as physical and they would be in charge of a number of under-gardeners and garden boys.

The first Maytham Hall of which there is any record was built in the mid-18th century and completed about 1760 by the Monypenny family, in whose hands it remained until 1890, when it was sold. It passed through a number of hands and was let to a number of tenants, including Burnett. "It was the old walled rose garden of the original Georgian house which inspired *The Secret Garden* and it was here that she met the robin which features so delightfully in her book." (from *Great Maytham Hall*, Country Houses Assoc. undated).

Allegedly the old entrance to the secret garden, now bricked up

The American writer and the English garden

The following sketches are from the same booklet.

1760
The Georgian house with coach
houses and walled garden behind,
and 'bothy' on the extreme right

1890
A second storey in pseudo-Gothic
style was added in about 1880

1900
The Hall was patched up after
the fire of 1893, with additional
windows.

There was a fire in 1893 which damaged the upper part of the house. It was repaired but after Burnett left, the house was sold to Harold Tennant, who had the building completely rebuilt between 1909 and 1911 by Edward Lutyens. Tennant was a Liberal politician and brother-in-law of the Prime Minister, Herbert Asquith. The house became a centre for gatherings of Liberal politicians until the First World War, after which the Tennants continued to live 'in the luxury of a bygone age' (*Great Maytham Hall*, ibid). It was used for various purposes during the Second World War, but the gardens were neglected and the house itself subsequently fell into disrepair. It was rescued by the Country Houses Association, restored and converted into fifteen flats, with residents sharing the reception rooms, entrance hall and drawing room; its first residents then set about restoring the gardens and grounds. The property is now owned by Sunley Heritage.

Maytham Hall c1907 (aka Maytham House and Great Maytham Hall)

Great Maytham Hall is unrecognizable after the Lutyens rebuilding.
The gardener's cottage can be seen on the far left.

The Millum family, George Snr, his wife Alice and the children Gert, George Jnr, Doris and Owen, left Rolvenden about 1910 and moved to St Johns, Woking. The reason for the move is unclear. it seems a big step to move from a familiar setting in Kent to what was then a distant West Surrey. The rebuilding of Maytham Hall may have been a reason but it appears that George Owen had already left Maytham Hall and was working at the nearby nursery, Maytham Gardens, as the testimonial overleaf from the owner shows.

"I have found him at all times… industrious, obliging & intelligent, with a good knowledge of his business & strictly sober & honest. He was, previous to Mr H. J. Tennant's ownership, in full charge of the gardens &, I believe, gave entire satisfaction to the… owners. We are very sorry to lose him & have every confidence in recommending him to any lady or gentleman requiring a hard-working gardener." Why Mr Tennant would want to lose such a gardener is mysterious, so perhaps it was George's decision, for some reason. He certainly left with plenty of goodwill from the staff, as well as a 'purse', as the

signed leaving card shows. Did Bertram Smith provide accommodation? If not, where did the family live?

Forty-five signatures follow, an indication of the number of staff
employed in a big house at that time. They could all sign their names
in good handwriting.

Flower shows were enormously popular and the owners of great
houses, or in Burnett's case the tenant, were extremely competitive.
Gardeners who could win prizes in the local show were much sought
after and sometimes poached from rivals. Both Rolvenden, the

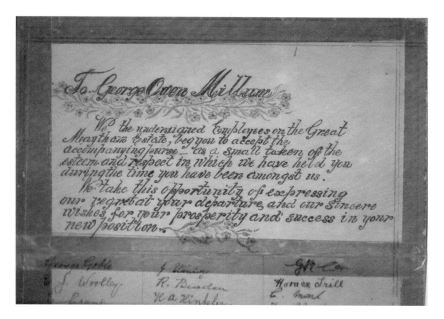

village where Maytham Hall was situated, and Tenterden, the nearest town, had flourishing 'Horticultural Societies' and accompanying shows.

George Owen was clearly a successful exhibitor at these local Horticultural Shows. This is just one of dozens of such winning labels.

George Charles Millum,
Son of The Secret Gardener

Whatever the reason, the family moved to St Johns Road, on the outskirts of Woking, presumably into another tied cottage. My father went to the Elementary School in St Johns, Woking. According to his school reports, which he kept, he seems to have been an above average student.

For the son of a gardener there was no likelihood of any further education and probably no desire for it at that point. Had he been born half a century later, the story would have been very different.

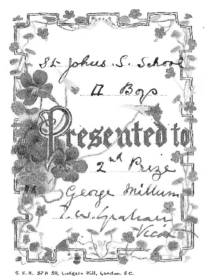

Dad followed his father (and his father before him) into gardening at the age of 14. Anyone with a medium-sized garden would employ a gardener, and the larger houses, of which there were many around Woking, were still employing many servants, even after the First World War. Being 'in service' was natural for George, as it was for his sisters, Gert, Doris and Rachel, who were to go on to work as cooks and nursery-maids in the area. The decline of the great houses and the employment they offered was a gradual, not a sudden process.

There are letters to Dad at a place called 'Rawdonly Lodge', St Johns Road, in which he is addressed as Master George Millum. Whether this is where the family lived or where he began working as a garden boy, in an unofficial kind of apprenticeship, is not clear. It wouldn't be unusual for a Head Gardener's son to be given work to learn the trade.

He certainly showed aptitude for the profession and was a good learner. By 1928 (aged 21 and with seven years' experience already) he was working at Dixon-Smith's Nurseries, Chobham, where he remained until made redundant in 1931, perhaps a consequence of the Depression. His diary entry for 24th January reads "Finished work at Marton [Dixon-Smith's] for good, after three years". At the beginning of January, he had written "Went after a job" so he probably had forewarning of the redundancy. A week after leaving Dixon-Smith's, he wrote "Started work. I don't think". The rest of the month has no entries, so he was obviously out of work. However, on March 2nd he started a new job at Braboeuf Manor.

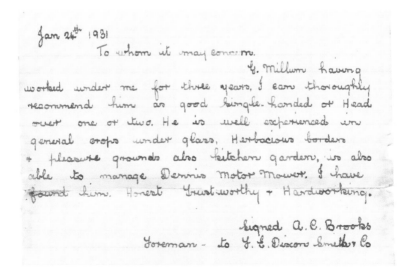

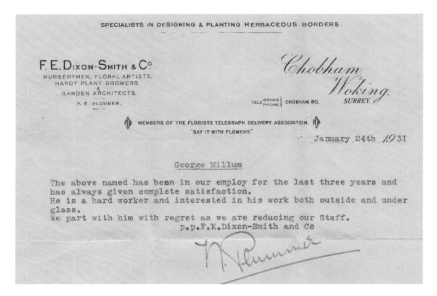

SPECIALISTS IN DESIGNING & PLANTING HERBACEOUS BORDERS

F. E. DIXON-SMITH & Co

NURSERYMEN, FLORAL ARTISTS,
HARDY PLANT GROWERS
&
GARDEN ARCHITECTS.

F. E. PLUMMER.

Chobham
Woking.

TELEGRAMS } CHOBHAM 80.   SURREY.
PHONE }

MEMBERS OF THE FLORISTS TELEGRAPH DELIVERY ASSOCIATION.
"SAY IT WITH FLOWERS"

January 24th 1931

George Millum

The above named has been in our employ for the last three years and
has always given complete satisfaction.
He is a hard worker and interested in his work both outside and under
glass.
We part with him with regret as we are reducing our Staff.
p.p.F.E.Dixon-Smith and Co

Braboeuf Manor, near Guildford, dated from the late 16th century and was surrounded by extensive gardens. It employed several gardeners, many of whom would be accommodated 'on site'. Unfortunately, any diaries from George's period at Braboeuf have not survived. I have nevertheless included information about the garden and his time there, as it gives an insight into the kind of life that he, and gardeners like him, would have lived.

"The grounds included a large area of parkland to the front of the house (to the east) and the matured pleasure gardens mainly to the south/south-west side. These contained, among other things, a rose garden, the sunken garden, two summer houses, the terraced garden, terraced lawns, the rock garden, the formal gardens, the kitchen and fruit gardens, the herb garden and the orchard and paddock. The rose garden was flanked by a pergola with brick piers (on the west side) and had a paved walk. The sunken garden contained a central lily pond, with stone paved surround and terraces. One of the summerhouses is in the corner of this garden.

The terraced garden adjoined the herb garden, and both of these led upwards to the southern boundary of the property and a thatched summerhouse. Attached to the Terraced lawns (on the south-west/ west side) was a small formal garden with a sundial, flanked by tall yew hedges. The rock garden contained a water feature with water flowing down from the high woodland through a number of pools and waterfalls. A path wound through the garden and a stone bridge crossed the water feature.

The formal garden is described as having stone flagged paths and clipped box edgings and the kitchen and fruit gardens as being extensive and stocked with vegetables and soft fruit. In 1947 there were also three Heated Greenhouses in these gardens.

Among the many separate buildings in the grounds were Squash Racquets Court, which measured 32 ft. by 21 ft. with a gallery and a changing room, Pound Cottage where an employee lived rent free, the Chauffeurs Flat, three garages, a workshop, two stores, and wood and apple stores, as well as many other buildings. A small pond is also shown on the very first Ordnance Survey maps (1871 and 1913) and in some photos, but is not mentioned on the sales particulars of 1947 (when the house was purchased by Felix Fenston Esq. after

Lt. Col J.A.C Youngers death). The gardens may have been partially designed by Gertrude Jekyll in 1907, but this idea is unfounded."

From Exploring Surrey's Past

(www.exploringsurreyspast.org.uk/themes/places/surrey/ guildford/artington_braboeuf_manor_and_gardens/)

The manor is described in Pevsner's Buildings of England 1971. It is now the administrative building for the University of Law, Guildford, who purchased it in 1964. (As an aside, Lt Col Younger's estate was worth £532,000 – approximately £20 million in 2021 values.)

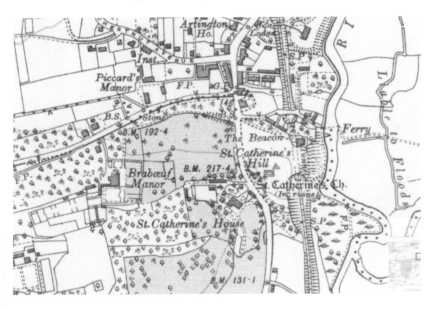

Letters from Dad to his brother Owen, who was in the Royal Navy, reveal an enjoyable bachelor life with plenty of friends and lots of contacts with family members. Some of the time he would have been living in the 'bothy' on the job and some of the time he spent time in lodgings in Woking, often sharing with one or other of his brothers, John and Fred.

George Charles Millum, Son of The Secret Gardener

I remember my Mum (the 'Winnie' mentioned in the letter) describing the bothy in tones of horror. "A frying pan thick with grease" was one of the phrases which has remained with me. I imagine that the young men sharing accommodation were not overly concerned with tidiness or hygiene. I was equally horrified on visiting one of the houses in which one of my sons lived while at university.

22/11/52.

Braboeuf Manor,
St. Catherines,
Guildford.

Dear Owen,

I haven't heard from you since you told me about that complaint of yours, but I expect that there is a letter on the way

Naturally I'm wondering how things are going with you - like, and I've only told John as he's the only one that wouldn't get the wind up - like.

I went up and saw Minnie this last weekend as my mate said that he'd do my duty for me, which was very good of him.

She was in bed all last week with a cold and a touch of rheumatism, but she's started work this week again and I'm going up this weekend. That any [...] keeps it dark.

Braeboeuf Manor,
St Catherines,
Guildford.

22/11/32
Dear Owen,

haven't heard from you since you told me about that complaint of yours, but I expect that there is a letter on the way. Naturally I'm wondering how things are going on with you like, and I've only told John as he's the only one that wouldn't get the wind up like.

I went up and saw Winnie this last weekend as my mate said that he'd do my duty for me, which was very good of him. She was in bed all last week with a cold and a touch of rheumatism, but she's started work this week again and I'm going up this weekend. Not arf. Keep it Dark.

I heard a bit of good news last week. You remember me being at Chobham at Dixon-Smith's? well, the lady has asked me if I would take on a job as Head Gardener over there at Hook Heath. She mentioned that there was a cottage, so if I thought of marrying (as I am) it would be just right. Of course, nothing is settled yet, but anyway, I'm hoping.

We are still playing squash here and I'm getting quite a champ. It's a good sport and keeps your fat down. Fred is still on the dole, but I think that he has a very good chance of a job at Woking next week.

I will let you know how things go in my next letter. Well, I'll say cheerio for this time, hoping to hear from you soon.

All the best – George

It was ironic that all the time George was writing to Owen, who had sailed out to New Zealand on board the HMS Dunedin, Owen was on his way back to England, to a hospital in Surrey. After many redirections, the letters eventually found their way back home. Owen was hospitalised at King George's Sanatorium for Sailors in Liphook, Surrey, presumably on account of the 'complaint' George mentions in his letter, but which is never given a name. Owen recovered and rejoined the Navy, only to die in the Second World War when his ship was torpedoed.

The Three Gardeners (George centre) and the Braeboeuf Manor's impressive gardens

In 1926 George joined the Territorial Army (318th Surrey Anti-Aircraft Searchlight Company) and became an enthusiastic member of the drum and fife band. He had a good ear and I remember his fife well, though he called it a flute. He would play marching tunes on it for our amusement and could also offer accompaniment to my Mum's piano playing on ukulele or an instrument, played with a bow, which he called a 'Japanese one-stringed fiddle'. It is, in fact, a phonofiddle.

He claimed to dislike spit and polish and the accompanying drill, but seemed to enjoy the TA. The story in the family was that he did it to get away from his domineering father but perhaps he joined along with a workmate for the adventure and a chance to visit somewhere different. His postcard from one of the jaunts does not have a very military ring: "Dear John, Well I have got here at last. All we did coming down here was sweat. I believe it is hotter than ever. Half a dozen of us were unloading the kitbags and of course one caught me swack on the napper. Hard luck, they said. Hard kitbag I said. Well this is all for now. Be good. From George."

On the back of a photo, he refers to 'Fred' as being in the same band; this is unlikely to be his brother, who would have been 12 when George joined and only 16 when the photo was taken. Going off to camp seems to have been seen as a holiday and a lark rather than a duty. Though, as the press cutting shows, he was pretty good with a rifle.

He continued in the TA when he moved to work for his next employer in 1933, but as there are no further records and no mention of absence at camp in the 1935 diary, it's likely he resigned when he got married and was moved to the Reserve, which was called up in 1939.

Dad with TA mate 'First turn out with the band 1930'

SEARCHLIGHT COMPANY'S PRIZE SHOOT.

Last Year's Champion Retains the Honour.

The 318th (Surrey) Anti-Aircraft Searchlight Company R.E. (T.A.) held their annual prize shoot at Pirbright ranges on Sunday, when about 80 members of the company took part. The day was brilliantly fine, and visibility on the ranges was excellent.

As in the previous year, the company was divided into three groups, class I being trained men and ex-Service men, class II second year recruits, and class III recruits. In class I the result was a tie between Sergt. J. Bazley and Sergt. S. J. Pigott. The contestants fired off another five rounds at 300 yards, the scores this time being Sergt. Bazley 17 and Sergt. Pigott 14. Sergt. Bazley is thus for the second year in succession the best shot in the company.

In class II the place for best shot was keenly contested, the result being Lance-Corpl. Farlie first and Spr. Millum second.

In class III Spr. Howard took first place and Spr. Willshire second.

On the whole the shooting was remarkably good, the high standard showing a considerable improvement over that of the previous year.

Luncheon and tea were provided by the company, and the members were conveyed to the ranges by the company's transport.

The prize-giving will take place at the annual smoking concert on November 15th. There are still a few vacancies in the company for the right type of man.

ABSENT FR...

Four Territ...

Four Territorials—... Friary-place, Guild... Thomas Leon...

TERRITORIAL ARMY or SUPPLEMENTARY RESERVE.

Army Form E. 654
(Pads of 50.)

NOTICE TO JOIN FOR TRAINING IN CAMP.

Name _Spr. G. C. Millum_

Number _2071633_ _R.E. T._ Regiment

YOU ARE HEREBY DIRECTED to attend at _Headquarters Sea Park Lane Guildford_ on _Sunday 5th August_ 19 _28_ at not later than _9.0_ o'clock a.m.

R.H.Elloy Trenchard Lt. R.E.(T.)

Date _1-8-28_
O.C. 318th (Surrey) Adjutant.
Search-Light Company Anti-Aircraft.

LEAVE OF ABSENCE from Annual Training in Camp can only be granted for most important reasons. Any such applications for leave must be received by the ... Men absent without leave are hereby warned that they are liable to be prosecuted against in the civil courts.

INSURANCE CARDS AND UNEMPLOYMENT BOOKS.—If you are insured under the National Health Insurance Act, 1924, and Widows', Orphans' and Old Age Contributory Pensions Act, 1925, immediately before training, you are required to bring your insurance card with you when joining for the annual training as directed above. You are also required to bring your unemployment book with you if you normally belong to an insured employment under the Unemployment Insurance Acts.

Promotion and marriage

In 1933 he did get the job mentioned in the letter and moved to work for Philip D'Ambrumenil at a house called Doiran, Hook Heath, Woking, as Head Gardener. He was quite young to have this position, though the gardening staff would have been relatively small compared to those in the grander houses and one suspects that by the 1930s fewer men were attracted to the life of 'service', even in times of recession. This was a fortunate step, as he had just become

engaged and the job came with accommodation suitable for a married man. 'Doree', 102 Kingsway, Woking, was owned by D'Ambrumenil and, unlike many gardeners' cottages, was in a suburban road a little way from the garden.

George married Winifred Mary Spicer from Forest Gate, London, on 25th January 1934. It was said that they met at Southend, and that Winnie went out with George's brother John to begin with.

CERTIFICATE OF COMPLETION OF APPRENTICESHIP.

I hereby Certify *that the within-named apprenticeship has been faithfully* served and completed this *31ˢᵗ* day of *October* 1930.

J. R. ROBERTS' STORES. LIMITED.

Managing Director. Signature of Employer.

Winnie left her employment at Robert's Department store in Stratford, East London, where she had completed her apprentice-

ship in 1930 to move to what was then a fairly rural environment. However, it was a move from a cramped terrace to a semi-detached house, though being next to the railway line turned out to be a disadvantage during the war as the junction at Woking was a target for German bombing.

They moved into the house in The Kingsway where they, together with my sisters, Patricia and Valerie, born in October 1934 and February 1937, lived throughout the war.

Dad (left) with brother John promenading in Southend

Valerie & Patricia

My mother, sisters and me

His new employer, Philip D'Ambrumenil, worked at Lloyds of London, of which he became Chairman in 1947. He was knighted in the New Year Honours 1945 for his services to the 'War Risks Insurance Office'. He also received honours from Belgium (Ordre de la Couronne) and Norway (Knight of the Order of St Olav - used to reward individuals for remarkable accomplishments on behalf of the country and humanity). How intriguing that an insurance expert should be awarded such honours.

Philip d'Ambrumenil

Head Gardener!

Unfortunately, there are no extant photos of the garden at Doiran. However, the garden diaries indicate that it was extensive: there are references to a croquet lawn, tennis courts, a kitchen garden and other areas of a substantial estate. His gardening diary for 1935 has survived and is the first of the two diaries transcribed in this book. After his death, my mum gave dad's collection of papers to me, being the historian in the family and knowing I was unlikely to throw anything away. It was only after retirement that I gave them the attention they needed and realised what a treasure trove they comprised.

The
Diary

George Millum, Head Gardener, 'Dorian', Hook Heath. Garden Diary 1935

The minutiae of day-by-day work will be fascinating to many gardeners. However, the lay reader may wish to dip in here and there or perhaps focus on the current month's entries. As the diaries were written in pencil and over the years have become smudged in places, some parts are hard to decipher. George's handwriting was excellent but not always easy to read, especially when the names of plants are unfamiliar. Another difficulty is the use of abbreviations. Frequently used references to areas of the gardens are these:

H.C. Hard Court
T.C. Tennis Court
K.G. Kitchen Garden
D.G. Dutch Garden
B.B.B. Bird bath bed
C.F. Cold Frame
House = Greenhouse/Glasshouse

Plant abbreviations are explained within the text as far as I am able. As far as possible I have used his punctuation, including the use of capitals, as written. Where words are illegible (or indecipherable (not quite the same thing) I have indicated thus ....

The dates given are the start of the working week, and the entries follow day by day and often include Saturday. This may have been a half day, but it is more likely that one or more gardeners would be on duty while others had the day off. Sometimes there are entries for Sunday. Living on the job, gardeners were expected to do whatever was necessary when it was necessary. I remember in the 1960s my dad cycling up to his place of work, two miles away, on a Sunday morning if the weather required greenhouse windows to be opened. Sometimes there was extra watering to be done – and who else was going to do it? You didn't want the plants you had nurtured to be damaged.

January

A gardener's job involved a lot more than looking after plants, especially as employers were beginning to have to make do with fewer staff. In January we see George looking after the woodland area, making soakaways and drains and laying crazy paving as well as ongoing tasks such as tennis court maintenance. A lot of time is spent making up displays for the house – making up bowls of tulips, for example, and vases of cut flowers. He was an excellent flower arranger.

The diary for 1935

Jan 1   Tree lopping
(Tues)   Ditto
           Ditto
           Ditto. Made up baskets with yellow tulips and primula.
           Raked back path border.
           Celery finished

Jan 7   Started Bonfire. Brought in box Tulip Mon Tresor, DVT
           [Duc van Tol] yellow, DVT scarlet. Made up bowl.
           Started raking woods. Fumigated G'House.
           Got bulbs out of ashes. Made up bowl.
           Woods
           Woods. Rolled H.C.
           Sweeping etc.

Jan 14   Woods. Got down 6 bags of ashes.
           Woods. Brought in 1 Sir Walton & 1 Golden Spear.
           Woods. Fetched in 6 Deutzias
           Woods. Made up bowl T., D.V.T., Y.
           [prob Tulips, Duc van Tol yellow.]
           Woods. Got down 6 bags of ashes.

Jan 21   FINISHED WOODS
Got out pine roots for new path.
Made soakaway. Put in two drains. Put down paving.
Paving.
Paving.
Made up bowl SJ. D V. T.S. *[prob Duc van Tol scarlet]*

Jan 28   Finished laying crazy paving.
Prepared ground under pine
tree for bricks.
Bricks laying.
Bricks.

February

The diary for 1935

February sees the start of a seemingly endless taking of cuttings: 300 chrysanthemum cuttings in the week beginning 4th February alone. It also sees the digging of trenches to plant celery, runner beans and peas. There must have been succession sowing of daffodils given that some are planted on February 5th and some cut on the 15th. Daffodil cutting went on till 8th April.

Feb 1   Bricks.
         Rolled H.C. Made up bowl & Basket. T.S.M.T.(V) & ST DVTS.
         [Tulip Mon Tresor - poss Van de Vinne - and more Duc van Tol.]

Feb 4   Finished Bricks. Got down 29 bags ashes.

The glasshouses were usually heated through a system of pipes fed from a coke boiler. Sometimes the same system fed the big house too. The ashes and clinker from the boiler were raked out and piles of these would accumulate. The ash would be used in the garden and as the diary shows, there was a lot of it. Coal or coke ash is rarely used today but cannot have been doing much harm to judge by the produce grown. It could have been helpful in retarding the onslaught of slugs and other pests. I remember heaps of pinky-grey ash alongside the boiler room which looked attractive to a kid but definitely did not lend itself to tunnelling or castle-building. My Mum discouraged it for some reason too.

Cementing Crazy Paving (cold). Made up Myosotis.

Planted rest of Daffs.

Took 240 Mum cuttings. Fetched out rest of bulbs from ....

Brought in 2 G. Spear, 1 Mon. T., 1 DVT & 1 S.W.

Took 60 Mum cuttings. Boxed up Dahlias, all excepting C.G.

[Chorus Girl?] & L.E. Picked out old Mum stools. Put in cold frame. Took 32 TR.GO *[Treasure Gold?]* cutts.

Finished cementing crazy paving. Sifted two lumps of ashes. Cleared up odd places.

Made up 2 baskets and 2 bowls.

Feb 11   Brought in 1 box Mon Tresor and 1 S.W.D. dug up rest of artichokes. Put pots on Rhubarb.

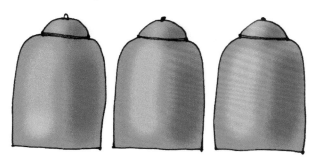

Top dressed rose garden with Superphosphate of lime

Sowed 3 pots of Toms, Sooted, weeded, trod and hoed Spring Cabbage. Dug artichoke bed.

Dug and manured Artichoke, Broad Bean and Early Pea ground. Got out 1 pea trench. Made up bowl of Hyacinths.

Got out 1 celery trench. Cleared off Savoy & odd greens stumps.

Got out 2nd celery trench. Picked Daffs & Freesias. Brought in box S.W., 1 T.C. D'Or, 1 T.D.V. T.S & E.D. Cut Daffs (bunches) and 1 Freesia.

Feb 18   Got out Runner Bean trenches.

Got out 2nd Pea trench.

Got out 3rd and 4th Pea trench. Wheeled 2 loads cow manure

Got out 5th pea trench and small trenches D.L. Sowed Peas & Broad beans & Artichokes.

The diary for 1935

Got out 6th Pea trench. Continued digging.

5 loads leaf mould came.

Wheeled in 4 loads cow manure. Digging.

(Sun)   Winter Gem Bronze

Feb 25   Looked over Mum cuts. Took 3 doz. Brought in 2 boxes of Hyacinths. Pot washing.

Started digging borders. Made up bowl. Took in two azaleas. Prepared boxes of Pots for Toms

Pot washing. Sowed Toms and 1 pot of Solanum. Digging.

Sowed lettuce. Continued borders.

Clipped Berberis. Tiddivated pine bed. Clipped Poly. Rolled H.C. & new turf. Went to Guildford.

Braeboeuf Manor, Dad's previous place of employment, was on the outskirts of Guildford and was easily reached by bus or train from Woking. Dad kept up social contacts with his old mates at the Manor until the war intervened and everything changed. The First World War, together with social change, had already had an impact on the bigger houses. There were fewer men available to do these jobs and fewer wanting to do them. Wages were low and though you were usually provided with accommodation, this would be lost if you were dismissed or wished to move. Some mechanisation (better mowers, for example) helped, but gardening remained (and remains) labour intensive.

March

Mar 4   *[Badly smudged entries this week]*

Started 2nd border, Brought in 3 Daffs, 1 Iris, 1 Hyacinth.

Continued on border. Sowed B Beans ... Lettuce, Radish ... put S.f. Mum ...Coleus.....

.... Lobelia ......

..... pruned laburnum ... continued borders ... made up two bowls.

Took in 5 Daffs & 1 Iris. Sowed .... Lettuce ....

The diary for 1935

Mar 11   Planted 3 carrots. Started on best border.

Potted up another batch of Mums.

Took Dahlia cuttings. Put bracken on B. Beans.

Took Fuchsia cuttings.

Got out No. 6 Pea trench and continued on border.

Took in 2 boxes daffs, 1 Hyacinth, 1 tulip, 2 Iris.

Put leaf mould on new shrubbery.

Continued on border.

Potted off another batch Mum cutts.

Took Hydrangea cutts.

Digging in K.G.

Sowed Primula, Ants & Solanum.

Finished border. Put 1 b. daffs

Put leaf mould on Rhododendrons etc.

Rolled H.C., T.C. and new turf. Spuddled over tulip beds.

Top dressed T.C. patches. Made group in front lobby.

Made up 1 basket and 3 bowls.

Took in 4 Daffs & 1 Tulip

(C.D'O), 1 Iris and 1 Peach blossom.

The term 'spuddled' or 'spuddling' occurs quite frequently. The definition can be somewhat vague.

This is from gardener Al Milway's blog, March 2005:

'I went out and had my first ever 'spuddle' at the weekend. It involved a bit of fork prodding, a little light trowel work, and even a few bits of weeding, but it was definitely a spuddle.

This word – or to give it its proper definition, verb – is something my family have used for eons to describe the lazy act of general attendance to your garden's needs. But it seems to meet the sarcastic tone of derision within my home. I'm sure that my cat would snigger, if he could, at my use of the word. It's not a real word! It's a silly yokel term that you silly Herefordians might use because you can't read to know the real term!

The fact that it doesn't have a dictionary entry does little to help my cause, but what better word is there for describing casual garden maintenance? Like pulling up a dandelion from the lawn, for example. Ok, so you could simply say 'I'm doing the gardening', but that's just so general it could mean chopping down a tree, or even more athletic and strenuous acts like digging a veg plot. And spuddling could never involve anything strenuous.

In fact there are a number of dictionary definitions online, which differ in stating the actions are trivial or purposeless. Definitely not the case here!

18 Mar   Took 112 dahlia cutts. Prepared ground for seed sowing (front drive). Sowed Brassicas etc. made up bowl Tulips. Planted gladiolas.

                 Cleared manure off Gladiolas. Top dressed tennis Court. 16 soil, 8 ashes, 2 soot, picked daffs. Sowed Grass seed front entrance.

                 Started top dressing front lawn. 8 barrows mixture. Prepared frame for Cauliflowers.

                 Nearly finished top dressing front lawn. Took Dahlia cuttings. Went over bird bath beds.

                 Finished top dressing front lawn. Altered group in house. Cleared off Dianthus in front of ......

                 Made up basket and 4 bowls. Picked daffs and Tulips. Made up bowl Hyacinths.

25th Mar Fumigated [Green] House. Took 7 doz Dahlia cuttings. Pricked out 6 boxes Lettuce. Sowed Peas L.S.&D. Got out pea trench. Sowed leeks and cauliflowers in frame.

Top dressed new turf and top lawn. Cut Daffs, Tulips & Forsythia.

Potted off Tomatoes in small 60's. Top dressing odd lawn. Picked Daffs.

Potted off Trigs. [Trigonotis, a type of forget-me-not]. Put first batch Mums outside. First batch Dahlias struck. Finished odd lawns. Planted Gladioli.

Weeded daisies near squash. Planted forced bulbs. Mulched shrubs on daffs border. Mulched Shrubbery. Took dahlia cuttings Remade Group in house. Made up 6 bowls and 1 basket.

April

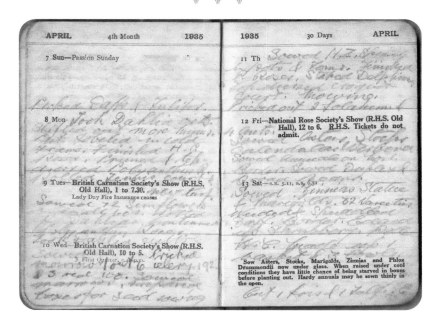

1 Apr 25 Umbellatum. Planted 50 Tigrinum Splendens 25 Croceum. [*all Lilies of different types*] Took Dahlia cutts. Potted off old stuff. Started Nepeta. Put out another batch Mums. Started pruning Roses. Pricked out 5 boxes blue Statice.

Cut coarse grasses and mowed Tennis Court. Roses. Finished Nepeta. Swept new grass.

Potted off old stuff. First batch of Dahlias. Mowing. Prepared seed boxes.

Shifted more Mums & Lettuce in cold frame. Fetched in 2 Iris 1 Tulip. Made up 1 bowl. Digging in K.G. Sowed Celery, Gourds, Penstemon & Statice.

Pot washing. Potted off odd stuff and took Dahlia cuttings. Finished mowing

Cold frames are used to extend the growing season at either end. They are used to get a head start on growing for the summer season by sowing annuals in them and they are a perfect transitional place for seedlings to get them ready earlier.

8 Apr Picked Daffs and Tulips. Took Dahlia cutts. Shifted out more Mums. Put Lobelia in cold frame. Finished H.P. Roses. Pruned and top dressed Polyanthus R. Rolled Tennis Court & new turf.

Sowed 72 Sunflowers in small 60's. potted off Dahlias, Polyanthus. Took Dahlia cuttings.

Sowed Marrow. Pricked out 6 Celery 192 & 3 red 100. Sowed Marrows. Prepared boxes for seed sowing.

Sowed N.Z. Spinach in pots and Toms. Finished P. Roses, staked Delphinium. Top dressed croquet court. Mowing. Pricked out 2 Solanum and 4 Ants.

Sowed Asters, Stocks, Calendulas & Verbena. Sowed annuals on No. 1 border. Sowed Duplex & Broad Beans.

Sowed Zinnias, Statice & Marigolds. 32 varieties. Weeded and spuddled Daff border. Edged up Shrubbery. Rolled H.C. Made up basket & 3 bowls. Cut 1 Iris and 1 Tulip. E.

The diary for 1935

14 Apr   Rolled T.C. & new turf. Sowing annuals. Potted off 120 Dahlias. Potted odd Mums.

Put old dahlia tubers outside except P.C.&P.M.J. Edged up rose garden. Cut Daffs, Iris, Tulips & Prunus bloom.

Potted off Gourds. Edged up all round. Took Dahlia cuttings. Went to Guildford.

Soaked Sowed Dwarf Beans. Cont. edging up. Put in Coleus cuttings. Potted off Torenia. Mowing.

Sowed Beetroot. Finished Edging up. Got in 1 load loam. Made up basket & 2 bowls. Prepared boxes for Celery. Cleared up bonfire.

Good Friday   One notes that George has Good Friday off but is working on Easter Sunday and the Monday. Having Friday as a holiday but working Sunday and Bank Holiday doesn't seem a very good deal. Looking at the previous weeks, he also seems to have worked Saturday and Sunday 13th – 14th April. It was only a five minute bicycle ride from The Kingsway to Hook Heath but I wonder if this work earned overtime. At this time George and Winnie's first child Patricia was just six months old.

Son of the Secret Gardener

Easter Sunday — Potted off 176 Dahlias & 188 Mums. 48's. Put Dahlias and Mums out in cold frame. Brought in 5 boxes Iris.

Planted out S.F. [*September Flowering*] Mums. Pricked out 14 boxes Zinnias. Got in flowers. Rolled paths. Cut first Spring Cabbage.

Prepared boxes for seed sowing and pricking out. 18 Zinnias, 30 Ants., 9 Asters, 6 Marigolds, 4 Calendulas. 102 boxes to date. Syringed greenhouse stuff.

Staked 6 small rows peas. Cleared off 2 rows brussels.

Mowing. Tied up creepers.

Mowing. Made up 2 bowls. Pulled first bunch radishes. C.F.

28 Apr — Digging in Kitchen Garden. Staked & top dressed 2nd border. Got in 2 loads cow manure.

Potting off rest of Dahlia cuttings. 100.

Put out first batch Ants in cold frame.

These will be Antirrhinums, more commonly known as Snapdragons and called that because their blossoms can be tweaked to open and shut like a dragon's mouth.

The diary for 1935

May

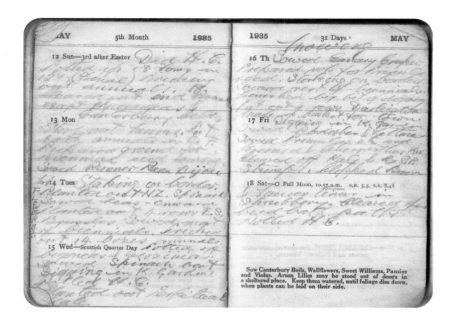

1 May	Potted up more Mums 48's. PREPARED HARD COURT FOR TOP DRESSING.
	Sowed Peas, Nemesia, Tagetes. Did a bit of edging. Top dressed H.C.
	Mowing. Made up 1 basket & 3 bowls. Continued on border. Hard Court finished. Staked Peas. Put more stuff outside in cold frame.
	Sowed 1 row S.E. Runner Beans.
(Sunday)	Put out another batch bedding stuff & Dahlias in C.H. Planted out Marrow. Sowed 2nd row R.B.*[runner bean]* Princeps.

6 May   Planted out last lot outdoor Mums. Preparing boxes for pricking out. Hoeing in Kitchen Garden.

Made up 3 bowls. Remade group flowers. Finished spuddling border No. 3. Pricked out 33 boxes annuals. Potted off Duc...

Top dressed Rose Garden. Potted off Coleus 60's. digging in Kitchen G. Cleared off B. Sprouts stumps and Broccoli.

Pricked off Primulas. Mowed. Got up Daffs and staked stuff on Daff border. Clear up in front drive.

Continued digging in K.G. Made up 1 basket & two pots Azaleas.

(Sunday) Did H.C. Potted up 18 Toms in 12's (Final). Pricking out annuals. Cleared out end bed except Hydrangeas & Canterbury Bells.

Flower pots were traditionally made from terracotta. They were made and sold by the cast, which is the number of pots produced from a given quantity of clay. So the tomatoes would be in pots with a top diameter of 12.5 inches (318mm) and would be 10 inches (254mm) deep. The coleus in 60s would be much smaller: 3 inches (76mm) diameter and 3.5 (89mm) deep. Other sizes commonly used were:

16s 9½ inches top diameter 9 inches deep

24s 8½ x 8

32s 6½ x 6

48s 4½ x 5

72s or thimbles c2½ x 2

80s or thumbs were even slightly smaller.

13 May	Stood out Mums. Put out batch annuals in C.F. Prepared ground for Biennial seed sowing. Sowed Runner Bean Bijou.

Staking on border. Planted out N.Z. Spinach. Sowed peas Onward. Planted out 4 rows E. S. Brussels. Sowed most of Biennials. Pricked out 14 boxes annuals.

Potted off Begonias and Gloxinias. Sowed Spinach beet. Digging in K. Garden. Rolled H.C. Planted out Perpetual Kale.

Mowing. Sowed Canary Creeper [*Tropaeolum peregrinum*] Prepared pots for Primula seed. Staking on border. Sowed rest of biennials. Finished big bit of digging. Put out 4 rows Darlington. Made up basket for town.

Digging in K. Garden. Sowed Radishes & Lettuce. Sowed Primulas etc and Veronica & Cheiranthus KW. Cleared off kale and B. Sp. Stumps. Clipped broom & Laurentias in shrubbery. Cleared off bird bath paths. Rolled H.C.

(Sunday) Fetched out 30 boxes annuals in cold frame. Rolled H.C. Prepared for pricking out. Sowed Marrows. Planted out Curly Kale.

20 May Pricked out Nicotiana Affinis 3, Asters 6. 30 boxes altogether. Sowed Golden Glenn Nasturtium. Cleared up wood heap.

Got out 6 rows Kale (Curly) 3 L.Q. & 1 V.S. PROCT. BRX. Weeded & pricked out annuals on L border. Cleared up Box heap.

OVAL BEDS Dig bird bath beds, Pine bed & Sque..... bed. Got up tulips in Azalea bed.

Mowing. Edged up all round. Weeded No. 2 border. Took in 2 Canterbury Bells. Staked Peas.

H.C. Did odd tying on border. Made up bowl flowers.

Staked Peas H.C. Rigged up another shelter for annuals. Sowed peas. Autocrat. Raked over Celery trenches.

(Sunday) 'Clotches' or cloches were made of glass and easily broken. Unlike terracotta pots the pieces were not easily reused as, for instance, aids to drainage. Quite what was 'rigged up' to shelter annuals, we don't know.

27 May   Staked peas. H.C. Rigged up another shelter for annuals. Sowed peas. Raked over celery trenches.

Pricked out last annuals 12 boxes Nicotiana, Nemesia & Ageratum. Weeding & pricking out, hoeing & staking and scrabbling over border.

Cleared up Lavender bed. Mulched. Planted out Broccoli 4 rows. Staked Toms. Syringed all round M.D.T. etc.

Syringed Ants in Toms, Planting out Savoys ...... Raked and weeded Rose garden.

Mowing. Staked R. Beans (2 rows).

Weeding & Hoeing in K.G. Cut grass round T. Court. Prepared soil for Mums. Put Marrows & Nasturtiums outside.

June

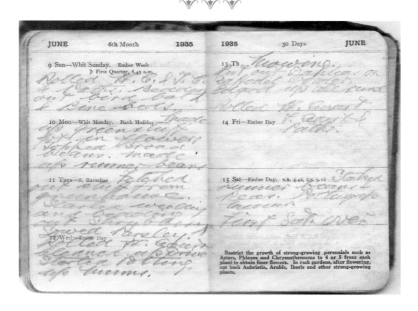

3 June   Hard Court.

Cleared out tulips in Dutch garden.

Planted out first batch Dahlias in new shrubbery. Clipping & hoeing in D. Garden.

Son of the Secret Gardener

Dug D. Garden. Bedded out oval beds. Planted out old Dahlia tubers.

Mowing. Trod D.G. Staking.

Bedded out Dutch Garden. Went round Herbaceous border.

(Sunday) Rolled H.C. & T.C. & paths. Bedded out bird bath and Pine beds

10 June Made up green stuff. Got in flowers. Topped Broad Beans. Made up runner beans.

Fetched out stuff from greenhouse. Started weeding & bedding out Shrubbery.

Sowed parsley. Rolled H. Court. Cleared up drive. Started potting up Mums.

Mowing. Put out Dahlias on Daffodil border. Edged up all round. Rolled H. Court, T. Court & paths.

The diary for 1935

[Friday 14th is blank]

Staked runner beans & peas. Potting up. First Sat over.

Some Saturdays were worked but not all. Is this reference to the first of a number of Saturdays to be worked?

The week following is very smudged:

(Sunday)   Picked peas

17 June   Rolled H. Court. .... Put out stuff in border
....
....
Sowed .... Cress, Radishes, Parsley, Carrots & Lettuce
Planted out Celery. Staking on borders. Flowers.
Picked B. Beans. Took in Peas, .., Lettuce, Radishes and Herbs.

24 June   Flowers. Bedding out No. 1 border. H.C.
Hoeing in K.G.
Did No. 2 border. Hard court
Did weedkilling.
Mowing. Staked No. 3 border
& bedded out. Marked out
court.
Staked & weeded Daffodil
border. Rolled H.C. & paths.
Flowers. Hard court. Marked
out court.

(Sunday)   Planted out last lot of green
stuff. (I hope) Planted out
leeks.

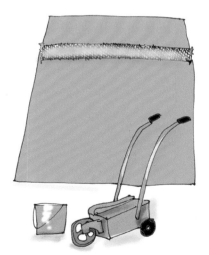

The 'I hope' in the last entry is a rare expression of feeling. Many garden tasks were boring and repetitive. My dad had an active mind and would often come home with puzzles, especially word puzzles, that he had worked on while weeding or bedding out or taking all those cuttings. He rarely told jokes but would frequently come out with a question such as, 'Mr and Mrs Shunnery had a son. What was his name?' (Dick, of course.) Though not sporty, he was keen on games and was often asked to organise them at parties. Christmas or family gatherings would be considered poor events without games and, often, sing-songs around the piano on which my mum played popular tunes from sheet music. My dad would accompany with the ukulele or one string fiddle and the rest of did what we could.

Made up by Dad, typed out (at work) by Pat, who made multiple copies with carbon paper.

S	A	C	(PIRATES' FLAG)
M	A	B	(MIXED BEER)
P	E	U	(REACH FOR THE SKY)
T	M	C	(PART OF PROVERB)
S	S	S	(TAKE YOUR PICK)
B	A	B	(ODDMENTS)
T	O	W	(EIGHT AGAINST EIGHT)
O	W	S	(TRAFFIC NOTICE)
N	Y	P	(WHAT WE'RE AT)
M	O	W	(BATTLESHIP)
J	B	J	(T.V. PROGRAMME)
S	A	P	(REPEAT)
F	I	L	(PATERNAL RELATION)
U	T	C	(AMERICAN CLASSIC)
T	G	P	(BOTTOMS UP?)
T	T	L	(THE END)

July

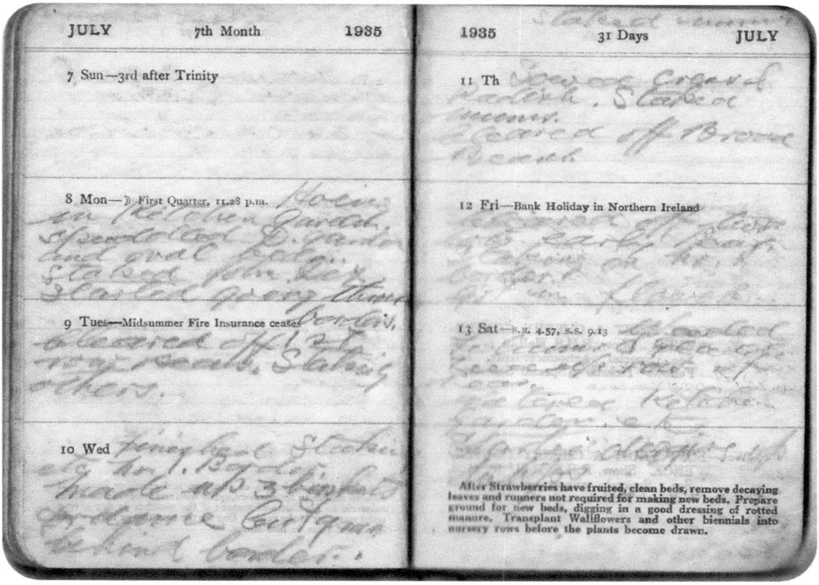
JULY
7th Month
1935
7 Sun—3rd after Trinity
8 Mon—☽ First Quarter, 11.28 p.m.
9 Tues—Midsummer Fire Insurance ceases
10 Wed
1935
31 Days
JULY
11 Th
12 Fri—Bank Holiday in Northern Ireland
13 Sat—S.R. 4.57, S.S. 9.13
After Strawberries have fruited, clean beds, remove decaying leaves and runners not required for making new beds. Prepare ground for new beds, digging in a good dressing of rotted manure. Transplant Wallflowers and other biennials into nursery rows before the plants become drawn.

July 1 Spuddled over Rose beds. Mowed tennis Court. Rolled H.C. and paths. Went round Delphiniums. Tying up.

Planted out box Zinnias and Stocks. Pricked out 950 Wallflowers etc.

Pricked out 3,000 biennials to date.

Cut creeper round windows. Mowing. Edged and weeded round croquet lawn. Raked under Pine tree (path).

Spuddled through B.B. beds, Pine bed and Rose G. strips. Edged up all round.

Plunged old greenhouse stuff. Staked peas.

Not as common as a tennis court, the croquet lawn was an embellishment to many large houses with sufficient space. Though not quite as demanding as a bowls green, the croquet lawn would have to be kept in good condition and without weeds, dips or bumps.

8 July Hoeing in Kitchen Garden. Spuddled D. Garden and oval beds. Staked John D. Started going through borders.

Cleared off 1st row peas.
Staking others.

Finished staking etc No. 1 border. Made up 3 baskets for dance. Cut grass behind border.

Staked Mums. Sowed Cress & Radish. Cleared off Broad Beans.

Cleared off two lots early peas. Staking on No. 2 border. Got in flowers.

Weeded. Tied up row of peas. Watered Kitchen Garden etc. started digging up tulips.

The diary for 1935

14 July   Got in flowers. Hoed Squash, back gate etc. Tidied up round bird bath. Started weeding & staking shrubbery.

Weeded Heather. Finished shrubbery. Digging up tulips. Finish second border.

Watered border & D.G. Continued on 3rd border.

Put out all odd stuff.

Watering Peas, beans & Celery. Cleared through drive. Syringed Dahlias in Dutch G. Mowing. Cleared off row of peas.

Got in Flowers. Dug ground (B. Beans) for pricking out. Finished staking on borders. H. C.

'In England, a 'Dutch garden' was the description given to a particular type of rectangular garden space, often enclosed within hedges or walls, even if part of a larger garden or parkland. This space would be laid out in a highly cultivated and geometrical, often symmetrical, fashion, shaped by dense plantings of highly coloured flowers, and edged with box or other dense and clipped shrubs.'
– Wikipedia

21 July   Get 1,000 Spanish Iris for borders.
Got both Courts ready. Flowers. Started cutting grass outside.
Finished grass.
Cut back hedge & shrubs round Squash.
Mowing. Watering D.G. Dahlias.
Edging up. Flowers.

28 July Picked first lot Runner beans.

Boxed up Tulips 1,200 & 400 mixed.

Watered dahlias. Cleared up No. 1 border.

Prepared soil for Primulas and Mums. Flowers.
Cleared up Daff border.

Raked over Rose beds. Cleared off 2

August

❦ ❦ ❦

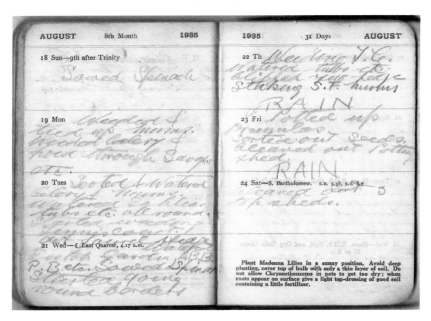

1 Aug Shifted Heap. Watered all round. Continued on No. 2 border.

Potted up Mums 32's. Finished border. Watered dahlias.
Swept woods. Tennis courts.

Flowers.

The diary for 1935

4 Aug   Went to Southampton.

5 Aug   (Bank hol)

Started No. 3 border. Box making.

Picked Peas & Beans. Finished border.

Beat Carpets.

Watered dahlias beds etc. Hoed biennial stuff, greens & Leeks

Watering in K.G. Picked up Daff bulbs.

The entry 'Beat Carpets' exemplifies the additional tasks a gardener might be expected to do in a house with limited staff, that is, to become an odd-job man. I can't imagine George was pleased to be doing this hard and dusty task, nor that it actually took the whole day.

11 Aug   Layered Carnations & took cutts.

Watering Dahlias etc. Hoed biennial stuff & Leeks.
Picking off blooms.

Cleared off Peas. Staked & tied up Dahlias.

Rubbing off blooms.

Rubbing off blooms. Watered long border & B.B.B.

Prepared ground for Spinach. Finished cutting off blooms.
Watered dahlias.

Hoeing in K.G.

18 Aug   Sowed Spinach.

Weeded & tied up Mums. Weeded Celery & hoed through Savoys etc.

Sooted & watered Celery & Mums. Watered Dahlias tubs etc. all round. Started weeding Tennis Court.

Cut Laurel Hedge. Watered Dutch Garden, B.B.B., P.B. etc. sowed Spinach. Started going round borders.

Weeding T.C. Watered tubs etc. Clipped yew hedge. Staking S.F. Mums.

RAIN Potted up Primulas. Sorted out seeds. Cleared out Potting Shed.

RAIN Cleared out 3 top sheds.

26 Aug   Top-dressed Mums. Started doing up Shrubbery. Cut off dead blooms in D. Garden. Sorted Sp. Cab. seedlings.

Finished Shrubbery. Tidied up B.B.B. Cut off dead blooms. Staked & tied up Mums.

Caught 33 earwigs. weeded & edged Rose garden. Mowing.

Finished Rose garden. Continued edging up & cleaning up.

RAIN Did drive and edging in front of house. Swept woods.

Cleared up in general all round.

Earwigs can be beneficial as they eat other pests such as aphids, but they can also cause a lot of damage. I remember my dad tying six-inch lengths of bamboo to the stakes holding the dahlias. The earwigs would hole up in there during the day. He would blow into one end of the tube and the earwigs would tumble out into a bucket of soapy water. I had unpleasant images of making the mistake of sucking instead of blowing. It's curious that in the entry above he should have counted them.

September

| SEPTEMBER | 9th Month | 1935 | 1935 | 30 Days | SEPTEMBER |

15 Sun—13th after Trinity. Ember Week

WORK.
10'8 816
3 6   3 6

16 Mon *Prepared soil and borer footballs.*

GALE.

17 Tues *Tied up crocker, got in flocked. Started wiring mums.*

18 Wed—Ember Day *Continued bulbs & mums. Staked Dahlias etc all round.*

19 Th—☾ Last Quarter, 3.23 p.m. *Cleared up rubbish on lawns. Potted Freesias.*

20 Fri—Ember Day *Finished evening mums. Continued getting in bulbs. Started papering celery.*

21 Sat—S. Matthew. Ember Day. S.R 6.42, S.S. 7.3
Got in flower.

Prune rambler and climbing Roses after flowering. Cut out as much of older wood as can be spared, and replace with the long shoots made this season. Many strong-growing Roses do well on their own roots. Select shoots which have flowered for cuttings, which should be about 8 inches in length. Remove lower leaves and plant firm 4 inches in sandy soil.

Son of the Secret Gardener

1 Sept	Arrived Southend 3. Raining. Went for walk. Saw some lights.

Holiday   Unfortunately, there are no further details about the holiday.
Holiday   Given that he and Winnie were recently married and had
Holiday   a baby, the most likely scenario is that they stayed at
Holiday   Winnie's mother's in Forest Gate. Southend was a popular
Holiday   holiday destination for people in that area of London.

16 Sept   Prepared soil & border for bulbs.
Tied up creeper. Got in flowers. Started wiring Mums.
Continued bulbs & Mums. Staked dahlias etc all round.
Cleared up rubbish on lawns. Potted Freesias.
Finished wiring Mums. Continued getting in bulbs. Started papering Celery.
Got in Flowers.

23 Sept   Man started on hedges. Dragged lawns. Started weeding lawns.
Continued weeding lawns. Covered up bulbs.
Continued lawns.
Cont. lawns. Mowing. Manured Dahlias.
Dug up Spiraeas (Back Gate).
Lawns.

30 Sept   Finished weeding lawns. Tied up & papered Celery. Cleared out Greenhouse.

Celery could taste bitter and one method of ensuring a better taste was to blanch (or bleach) the stalks after the plant had grown to a height of 18 inches or so. This can be done by earthing up or by wrapping paper around the stems. In a few weeks the stalks will be pale and can be cut. This technique seems to be less common today, perhaps as new varieties of celery have been bred. However, there is at least one YouTube video showing how to do it.

The diary for 1935

October

| OCTOBER | 10th Month | 1935 | 1935 | 31 Days | OCTOBER |

13 Sun—17th after Trinity

14 Mon—Michaelmas Fire Insurance ceases

15 Tues

16 Wed

17 Th

18 Fri—S. Luke

19 Sat—☾ Last Quarter, 5.36 a.m.   s.r. 6.29, s.s. 5.1

Plant Roses, fruit and other deciduous trees and shrubs. Now is a good time to plant or renovate herbaceous borders while the soil is still warm.

1 Oct   Continued Celery. Rest of bulbs came, started boxing.
Clipped Lavender in shrubbery. Finished Celery.
Finished getting in bulbs. Made up three bowls.
Planted up Lavender. Dragged lawns.
Got in flowers.

7 Oct   Started clipping shrubbery.
Put H.C. Right. Got up
Fuchsias etc & potted up.

Continued shrubbery.
Potted up 100 Carnations.

Clearing up Shrubbery. Transplanted shrubs, Lilacs etc.

Cleared off Dutch Garden. Got up Gladiolas washed and put in house.
Made up bowl & vase. Put out row Spring Cabbage.

14 Oct   Springboked T.C. finished Lavender bed, transplanted and cleared up Heather.

Patched T.C. and Square. Burned up Rubbish. Cleared off B.B.B. Pruned climbing Roses.

Earthed up Celery. Continued Roses.

Cleared up path near Rose Garden. Cut creeper round house. Got in Flowers.

Cleared up leaves on T.C. & round about.

Cut Blanche Poiteau. [Pear] FROST No 1

21 Oct   Got Mums inside except W.F.B., W.O. & W. Gem. Cleaned Gladioli corms. Got in Flowers. Potted up C. Bells & Sweet William.

I'm grateful to Roger Brownbridge, President of the National Chrysanthemum Society, for suggestions as to these varieties: "WFB - this would appear to be W F Barton, a red October flowering large intermediate raised by Shoesmith. W Gem - here there are two options: White Gem, a white September flowering medium intermediate, or Wisley Gem, a bronze September flowering pom-pom. WO - my only finding on this one was Worthing Orange, a November flowering light bronze intermediate."

Made up Gourd bowl & Berry Basket. Dug up and washed Paisley Gem. Packed.

Got up Cotinus Gem. Started on .... Vars.

Swept up leaves on lawns. Rolled H.C. Flowers. Dragged lawns.

Finished digging Dahlias & washing. Planted daffodils. Squash Court. Potted up 3 outdoor mums.

The diary for 1935

This is the first mention of a squash court. What was done to it? Perhaps it was open to the weather and needed sweeping and so on. Dad was certainly aware of squash as a sport and played it in his younger days. Or is it a slip of the pencil for 'Squash bed'?

27 Oct   Cut Cucumber Egremont 3

        Packed rest of Dahlias. Mowing. Gourd bowl flowers etc.

        Put bone-meal on Croquet Court. Dug and manured Squash bed. 4 loads manure came.

        Bone-mealed big lawn. Dug, manured and reshaped oval beds.

        Dug bird bath beds. Oval beds. Picked over and disbudded Mums. Rain.

November

❧ ❧ ❧

NOVEMBER 11th Month 1935

3 Sun—20th after Trinity. ☽ First Quarter, 11.12 p.m.

4 Mon

5 Tues—Show, R.H.S. Hall, 1 to 5.

6 Wed

1935 30 Days NOVEMBER

7 Th

8 Fri

9 Sat—S.R. 7.5, S.S. 4.22

Prune all kinds of fruit trees, except Gooseberries and Red Currants, where birds are troublesome, when they should be left until March. Take out the old fruiting wood of Peaches and Nectarines leaving sufficient young shoots to take their place, but defer tying in young shoots until end of February.

1 Nov   Fetched in Greenhouse 5 boxes Iris. Dug Dutch Garden beds.
Flowers. Did Berry basket, gourd bowl & bowl (sic).
Clearing up leaves off lawns.

3 Nov   Cut Mohawk 2 or 3 P Bernier 2 nat. Romance 2 nat.
Superbum Single Cr...... November Sun 2 P Fantasy 2 nat.

Planted Tulips & Myosotis in Oval beds. Finished digging D.G.
Cleared off Azalea bed.

Staked standards on daff border. Trod B.B.B. Planted Roses near
Squash.

Planted Wallflowers in B.B.B. Trimmed up & planted Berberis in
Shrubbery (HALF). Fumigated Mums.

Got in flowers. Continued Berberis. RAIN Went over Mums for Leaf Miner.

Made up G. bowl & bowl & vase. Birmingham.

10 Nov   Cut Golden Seal. ....

Got in, staked & tied up Freesias. Planted Tulips in Squash bed. Planted rest of Berberis.

Got Iris out of ashes & put in frame, also Soleil d'Or. Shifted shrubs in shrubbery.

Got in and cleaned Sweet Williams. Edged up shrubbery. Got in flowers.

Trod & raked over D.G. Finished planting shrubs in shrubbery.

Springboked shrubbery. Started turfing bank.

Got in flowers.

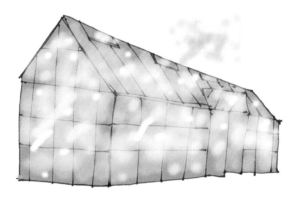

17 Nov   During last week. Dec. Gold 1

Finished turfing bank. Rolled H. Court. Planted half D.G. with Tulips. Fumigated 'House.

A greenhouse would be fumigated to clear out any pests before the winter or that might be over-wintering e.g. red spider mite, whitefly and aphids. It's likely that my Dad used a sulphur candle which was

placed on a heat resistant surface in the middle of the greenhouse. All the windows were closed, the wick was lit and the gardener retired smartly. The greenhouse would be left for twelve hours and then ventilated thoroughly. There are environmentally friendlier alternatives available now.

Cyanide was also used as a fumigant. It wasn't always entirely safe, as my great-grandfather discovered in 1916. He perished from 'From a dose of Cyanide of Potassium accidentally taken'. The family story was that he confused the poison with one of his bottles of home-made liquor.

Rank or Profession.	Cause of Death.
Gardener	*From a dose of Cyanide of Potassium accidentally taken. Accidental death.*

Finished Tulips in D.G. Planted odd ones all round.

Put peat & Sweet Williams in Rhod. Bed. Planted Chiranthus in strips.

Gourd bowl. Got in flowers. Dug up S.F. Mums & put in frame. Planted out Aquilegia, Verbascums, C. Bells.

Sweeping up on lawns. Fetched out Paper Whites from house to frame (in bud) Emptied tank.

Made up bowl.

24 Nov   Start was made on Rose Garden.

Raked up in Pine trees. Spuddled back of daff border. Took out Mum stools in cold frame. Brought in last lot of Mums.

Cleaned up front of Daff borders. Planted S.W. & Linum. Weeded D.G. paths.

Started on bottom border. Put bone meal on T.C., shrubbery & odd places.

Got in flowers. Continued on border. Planted S.W. in Rhodo bed. D. MxD.

Continued on border. Finished bone-mealing.

Bone meal is an organic fertiliser comprising a mixture of finely and coarsely ground animal bones. It's a slow-release fertilizer used primarily as a source of phosphorus and protein. Grass on tennis courts would usually be fed in spring, so its use here is curious.

December

DECEMBER 12th Month 1935   1935 31 Days **DECEMBER**

2 Dec   Cleared up rubbish under Pines. Started clearing long border.

Wheeled in 2 loads C.P. Got in Azaleas and Deutzias. Continued on long border.

Shifted Soleil d'Or in house from ashes to frame. T.D.V.T.S & T.D.V.T.Y. Golden Spear King Alfred. Finished bottom border.

Fetched in primulas & Hydrangeas. Tidied up S.W. & C. Bells. Edged up gravel path. Raking grass behind Bottom border.

Started preparing ground for heather front gate. Finished grass behind border. Cleared up leaves round Croquet Court & Tennis Court.

Cut W.G. Winter Cheer, Valerie, K.O.T.P. Biennial & B.B. Pinch apr. (Trial)

The diary for 1935

8 Dec First few Iris in bloom.

Planted Ericas F.G. Potted some up for Xmas blooming. Continued on long border. Planted 250 Iris. Went over Mums.

Got in flowers. Finished cutting down on long border. Wheeled in 2 loads stable manure. Put on Rhubarb, Celery, Artichokes etc.

Finished long border. Started cutting down on short border.

Finished cutting down on short border. Cleaned up half.

Shifting furniture(?) border. Did odd sweeping. Made up everlasting vase.

Made up 2 vases. Pats Party. Cut 30 Iris & Mums.

Given that this entry is on a Saturday, perhaps this is a Christmas party for daughter Pat - at two years old, it's a possibility.

16 Dec Brought in 8 Paper Whites. Finished borders. Cleared up one side of drive.

Started clearing other side of drive. Cut 1 bunch Iris.

Finished drive. Edged & cleared up croquet court.

Cleared up rubbish dump in Kitchen Garden. Painting buds.

Flowers. Made up 2 pots for lobby. Made up basket. Got Xmas tree. Made up gourd bowl & Hat (sic).

23 Dec Raking behind Heather. Got in flowers. Iris, Paper Whites & Mums. Covered up Celery & Laps

Continued Raking.

Christmas Day /

Boxing Day

27 Dec   Squash & Hard Court

30 Dec   Took first batch Mum cuttings & plants. Brought in Iris
Wedgewood. Soleil d'Or in bloom. Mon Tresor & Prince of
Austria. Took D.V.T.S & Y inside house & 3 Hyacinth.

The war years and beyond

Dad continued working for Philip D'Ambrumenil at Doiran until 1941. A note written in D'Ambrumenil's handwriting suggests that he was hoping to get George exempted from call-up on the basis of producing food, which was a reserved occupation. It seems that Dad would then use his employer's words to complete his own application.

Son of the Secret Gardener

'I am head gardener at Dorian Hook Heath Woking. My employer is Mr P D'Ambrumenil, Wyngates, Hook Heath Woking. Dorian is owned by Mr D'Ambrumenil & has a considerable vegetable garden which is being further extended. The vegetables are for the use of Mr D'Ambrumenil & his family at Wyngates Hook Heath Woking & for the office staff at present at Dorian as well as the gardeners. My employer was advised to apply for postponement to the Surrey Home Agriculture Executive Committee, which I am assured he has done...' The reverse contains three lines partly indecipherable but which include 'a wife and two children ... dependent on my wages'.

There would seem to have been a postponement, as his Record of Service shows 17/7/41 to 29/3/46.

Eventually Dad was called up to serve with a Royal Artillery Anti-Aircraft Company presumably because of his Territorial Army involvement. He was based at a series of camps around the UK, from Kent to Cornwall. His experience stoking the boilers of the great houses (a subsidiary job for many gardeners) stood him in good stead. A typewritten note of 1942 states that 'The following are Cooks and boilermen who are of no use as Gun Nos., but are of great value in the capacity in which they are at present employed' and lists a Millum, D.J. Boilerman. There was no D J Millum so this must be a clerical error as the Army No. (1804390) is correct. The 'no use' is interesting as Dad always said he was taken off anti-aircraft gun duty as he couldn't stand the noise. It was probably fortunate that he had boiler stoking and management experience or his wish might not have been so readily granted. The work entitled boilermen to come on parade in their fatigues, which meant he was also excused the spit and polish of the parade ground inspection, something which pleased him enormously.

Being home-based, he was able to get leave to return to Woking fairly often. In between, he and Winnie wrote many letters and there was the odd telegram, this one for Winnie's birthday in 1942.

In spite of air-raids, morale at home seems to have been good. The letters from the girls to their Dad are remarkably cheerful:

Dear Daddy. I hope you are well I am looking forward to your 7 day leave. So is Valerie. We had an ice cream When you went back. Mummy bought us a Writing book each and a bag of mixed chocolates and a bag of nut chocolates. I am Writing this letter in bed, if theres an airraid I am going to get under the bed and play marbels or ball under  mummys bed of cause. I must say cheerio for now love from Patricia Doris Millum There you are my Peach Blossom xxx

I was born in September 1945, a month premature, but healthy enough.

Dad sustained a war wound while at the Wormwood Scrubs base in July 1942. 'Gnr. Millum was cutting a piece of an inner tube to make a rubber washer for a water tap; whilst doing this the knife slipped and cut his finger. Gnr. Millum is a good and reliable soldier, and although it appears that he might have been a little more careful, I would not say that it was due to gross negligence.' The M.O. remarks '1 stitch inserted. Not severe. Unlikely to interfere with his future efficiency as a soldier.'

55909   Army Form X 202/B.

CERTIFICATE OF TRANSFER to the ARMY RESERVE

Army No. *1804390*   Rank *GNR*

Surname (Block letters) .... *MILLUM*

Christian Name(s) .... *George Charles*

Regt. or Corps ... R.A. (H.A.A.)

The transfer of the above-named to the appropriate Class of the Army

Reserve (see note below) is confirmed with effect from *30 MAR 46* .

*The date to be inserted here will be that following the day on which Release Leave terminates, including any additional leave to which the soldier may be entitled by virtue of service overseas.

Note.—The appropriate Class of the Army Reserve is as follows :—

(i) Royal Army Reserve—in the case of a regular soldier with reserve service to complete :

(ii) Army Reserve. Class Z (T)—in the case of a man of the Territorial Army, including those called up for service under the National Service Acts :

(iii) Army Reserve, Class Z—in the case of all other soldiers not included in (i) or (ii) above.

Record Office Stamp.

R. A. RECORDS
HE A . . A.
5 MAR 1946
R U G B Y

.... for Colonel,
Officer i/c I/s R.A. Records, Heavy A.A. Records.

Date ....

Warning.—

Any alteration of the particulars given in this certificate may render the holder liable to prosecution under the Seamen's and Soldiers' False Characters Act, 1906.

If this certificate is lost or mislaid, no duplicate can be obtained.

Wt. 37285/96   1,000M   12/45   KJL./1516/16   Gp. 38/3

He was demobbed in 1946, but D'Ambrumenil had moved to Sunningdale, to a smaller property, and no longer needed a gardener. His letter explains that their new garden is not large enough to require a gardener, so new employment had to be found – and, with it, accommodation.

My Dad had a good deal of respect for D'Ambrumenil, which was, I think, reciprocated. He had less time for some of his other employers, including the next one.

Bankside House,
107-112 Leadenhall Street,
London, E.C.3.

8th February, 1946.

Mr. G.C.Millum,
    "Doree",
      102 Kingsway,
      WOKING,
        Surrey.

Dear Millum,

    With reference to the conversation I had with you, as arranged I have given instructions for the discontinuanc3 of the allowance of 15/- a week which has hitherto been paid to you.

    With regard to the house, I told you that I would allow you to stay for the time being without any payment of rent, it being understood that you would vacate when I asked you to do so. For the moment at least, I shall not ask you to pay the rates.

    I sincerely hope you will get a job after your own heart and only regret I do not now have a garden which makes it possible for me to re-employ you. I do, however, thank you for all you have done for me in the past and I hope that the time will arrive when I shall be able to say to you – "Do you want to return to me".

    With all good wishes,
        Yours sincerely,

A new position

His next employment was at Trevarno, on the Hockering Estate, at the other side of Woking, where he worked for a Major du Boulay. The gardener's accommodation, Trevarno Lodge, was outwardly fine but suffered from chronic damp. My mother remembers mould on the table legs! Although du Boulay was not popular with us, it seems that the other family members were friendlier and we three children were allowed to play in the grounds. For whatever reason, the job did not last long, for in 1948 we moved again. Dad's new employer was Evelyn Ricks, a successful builder and developer, who lived at Horsell Grange, on the road to Chobham. The gardener's cottage, Horsell Lodge Cottage, was not damp but it was a poor comparison with 102 Kingsway. There was no kitchen, only a 'scullery' which also accommodated a copper and a bath. The copper was lit every Friday and the hot water ladled into the bath. Yes, we did share the bathwater. There being only two bedrooms, I shared the larger one with my sisters. It was a happy place to grow up in as I had the gardens and woods of the adjoining Church Army Old People's Home to explore and play in. But the house was small and much of our furniture had to be stored. It was kept in a little wooden building two hundred yards

Horsell Lodge Cottage

away which was called Rookery Nook. The piano and the three-piece suite had to be stored there as well as other items of furniture, all of which irked my Mum considerably. Pat used to practise piano there and there were musical evenings, too.

Mr Ricks had a large garden over the road at Horsell Grange, though Dad was the sole gardener. In a fairly short period, Dad had gone from being one gardener of several in a huge garden to being the sole gardener in a more modest property, and from 'Head Gardener' to mere gardener, though this did not seem to bother him. It also reflected the trend of the times. Between the First and Second World Wars, the gardens of many great houses had struggled on, often with fewer staff. By 1945, the larger gardens were often neglected or had been turned over entirely to food production. Extensive gardens with the staff needed to maintain them were increasingly rare.

Horsell Grange

Dad's diaries from 1949 and into the 1950s have survived. They describe in detail his work at Horsell Grange's garden, which, though much smaller than Braboeuf's or Dorian's, seemed very big to me as a child when I went to 'help my dad'. I have chosen the diary for 1949 to be transcribed in this book.

A new position

Horticultural shows were very popular and there was a lot of competition for prizes. Mr Ricks won many prizes at the Woking Show, though the actual gardener was, of course, my father. As well as the garden diaries, I found in his collection of documents and memorabilia, over 70 winning tickets from horticultural shows (or 'flower shows' as they were known). These cover the years 1949, 1950 and 1951, during which time he also won (on behalf of E Ricks) four 'Challenge Cups'.

Dad with trophies outside Horsell Lodge Cottage
Below: two of the many prize tickets

In 1954 my mother in particular was delighted to move from Horsell Lodge Cottage to a council house on the south side of Woking on Barnsbury Farm Estate.

Our new house, christened *Patrevale*, was a long way from Horsell Grange, which may have been the reason that Dad left Mr Rick's employ. After a short interval working elsewhere, he was employed once more on Hook Heath, Woking. The first job was for a Miss Bennett and latterly for a family called Archibald, who ran a prep school called Allen House School.

Horsell Grange

He was working here up until his death in 1974 at the age of 66. The school continued for a while longer but is now an area of expensive housing called Allen House Park.

My father was a smoker of unfiltered roll-you-own Digger Shag tobacco. This, together with the fumes from the many coke boilers he stoked and his exposure to so many virulent pesticides, may have contributed to the lung cancer from which he died.

George Millum, Gardener, 'Horsell Grange', Woking. Garden Diary 1949

January

Jan 3rd   Wheeling out compost K.G. Shifted pear trees.

Went over carnations and through greenhouse stuff.

Picked mums. Xmas Red, Xmas Gold and Sunset Pink.

Picked first Freesias.

Prepared soil for Mum cuttings.

Took Mum cuttings. Trimming up Rhods in drive. Got out currant bush.

Trimming round Rhods in drive. Levelling heather turf bank.

Finished turf wall and dug border. Got up plants for Dr.S.*

Got heather from Nursery. Sweeping up etc. Took in Azalea and two Cinerarias this week.

*Dr. S was almost certainly Dr Smellie, our family doctor. My dad did some gardening for him and he became something of a benefactor, even offering to lend us c. £300 in 1946 when we were about to lose the tied house in the Kingsway as Dad moved jobs. The offer was turned down as my mum and dad didn't want the worry of debt and, perhaps, of maintaining a house. In hindsight, this seems a shame as the house would have appreciated enormously. But at the time £300 was a lot of money and there was no history of home ownership in the family. Sometime later, Dr Smellie removed my tonsils and my appendix and saw me through various childhood illnesses.

Jan 10th   Wheeling out manure on herbaceous border.
Raking leaves under archway. Planted Ericas in strip.

Straightening Ericas in drive.

Straightening Ericas in drive. Planted polyanthus in strip.
Fumigated house.

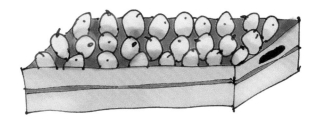

Took 4 pots Car[nation]. Cuttings. Boxed new potatoes to sprout.

Took down rose poles in H border*. Cleared out mower shed.

Went through G house stuff. Sowed cauliflower Forerunner
Sprayed orchard 18 galls mxd Universal.

Sweeping up etc.

(poisoned rats)

*H border – herbaceous border. Given the amount of time spent on it, the herbaceous border must have been sizeable.

Jan 17th   Planted small pear. Dug up 2 roots rhubarb. Transplanted
Thyme. Moved 10 Rhododendrons.

Spraying fruit trees. Shifting shrubs in border.

Shifting shrubs in border. Pruning etc.

Planted polys and N.T.s in centre bed. Planted roses, P's and H.T.'s [*hybrid tea roses*].

Sweeping up etc.

Jan 24th   Looked over stuff in shelter. Planted rhubarb. Started patching lawn.

Patching lawn.

Patching and levelling lawn.

Finished lawn. Edged shrub border. Raised path round house.

Edged triangular bed. Tiddyvated* rose beds and borders round house. Weeded rockery and cleared off leaves from polyanthus.

Sweeping up etc. Fumigated house.

Jan 31st   Wheeled out 18 barrows compost. Fruit trees K.G. etc. Went through frames. Shifted half Sp Cab [*spring cabbage*] bed. Preparing for paths.

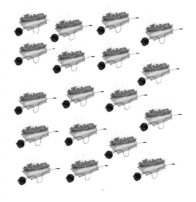

*'Tiddyvated' would seem to be Dad's version of titivated, meaning 'to make oneself look smart or to improve small details'. His spelling of the word does occur in the Slang Dictionary of the Turf by John Bee, 1823. 'i. e. made tidy, or neat; derived from Nitida, neat, tidy, spruce, genteel, prim, gay. Used by barbers and friseurs for a drest head formerly; but now confined to lasses and dandies who may have emerged from a recent state of filth, after adonising their persons an hour or two.' (adonising – from adorn.)

February

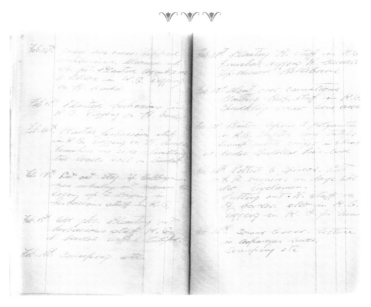

Feb 1st Brought down lachenalias from shelf. Cleared out propagating frame. Took 6 pots cuttings (mums) and 2 Cars.

Shifted and split up 2 peonies in Dahlia border. Started clearing out and digging H border. Wheeling out compost for Dahlia borders.

[14°F] Pruned Pyrocanthus and Wisteria in H border. Digging H border.

[17°F] Raking up leaves by front entrance. Cut back Cydonia [quince] and buddleia.

[16°F] Sweeping up etc.

Temperatures are mentioned from time to time, usually to record degrees of frost. A maximum and minimum thermometer would always be kept in a greenhouse and there would probably be others. 14°F = -10° Celsius

The diary for 1949

Feb 7th   Took pot coleus cuttings. Sowed box cress. Cleared leaves from Dahlia border. Pruned roses along cottage.

Put fuchsias in cold frame. Wheeling out compost.

GALE Sowed lettuce, carrots and peas. Cloched peas. Took cuttings of Per. Mum. Digging on H border.

Sowed tomatoes, Mustard and Verbena. Digging on H border.

[12°F] Digging on H border. Planted 25 roses in K.G.

RAIN Sowed salad lettuce, ... and celery. Pricked out box lettuce. Sweeping etc.

Feb 14th   Sowed box cress. Tipped raspberries. Cleared up coke pit. Planted aquilegia and phlox in K.G. Digging on H border.

Planted herbaceous in K.G. Digging in H border.

Planted herbaceous stuff in K.G. Digging on H border. Finished one side. Levelling two loads soil in border.

Put out Sp. Cabbage. Wheeling out manure. Digging up and laying in herbaceous stuff in K.G.

Odd jobs. Planting out herbaceous stuff in K.G. and border. Daffs and tulips.

Sweeping etc.

Feb 21st   Planting H stuff in K.G. Finished digging H border.
Top dressed hellebores.

Went over carnations. Planting Herb. Stuff in K.G.
Spuddling under vine arch.

Planted lupins and polyanthus in K.G. Shifted some tulips
Transplanted conifer in shrub border. Spuddled iris bed.

Potted 6 spiraeas. Put 30 F.R. begonias in large 60's also cycla
Putting out H stuff on H border. Also in K.G. Digging in K.G.
for mums.

Sowed cress, lettuce in asparagus beds. Sweeping etc

Feb 28th   Planted out Delphs and lupins in K.G. Sowed Mustard. Put in
12 pots mums. Spuddled in K.G. Laid in leeks and rest of celery.

March

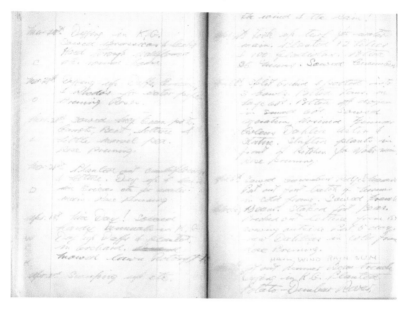

The weather is not often mentioned but this week is exceptional with wind, rain and snow noted.

Mar 1st WIND! Put in box lettuce (Arthur). Mowed lawn with spinner.

Dug Dahlia border. Planted arbutus. Spuddling up through bush apples.

Spuddling borders in drive. Put in pot of Car. Cuttings in new stuff. RAIN Potted orchids. Pricked out cauliflower, ... Took two pots Car cuttings. Potted Coleus and Cactus. Sowed celery and toms. Planted asparagus.

SNOW Sweeping etc.

Mar 7th   Spuddling borders on drive. Top dressed currants, manure and prune down.

Planted azaleas in centre bed. Spuddling borders on drive.

N E WIND Sowed Mustard and Cress. Spuddling borders on drive.

Mulched newly planted rhubarb. Mixed soil for seed sowing. Finished spuddling borders on drive. Put out rest of Herbaceous stuff on border. Spuddling Hypericum bed.

Prepared site for Rhododendrons. Split up old Mum stools.

Sweeping etc.

Mar 14th   RAIN Splitting up old mum stools, potting etc.

Potted old geraniums etc. Sowed Beet, Carrot, Peas, Lettuce, Spinach, Onions & Celeriac.

Sowed Velocity Cabbage, Cauliflower & Brussels. Dug palets (?) in K.G. Manured from 3rd bay.

Planted out forced bulbs. Potted 12 Tomatoes 72's. Planted shrubs (new) also new herbaceous stuff. Potted 12 new outdoor mums.

Planted new herbaceous stuff, Iris, Astilbes etc. Spuddled between raspberries. Top-dressed asparagus with salt*.

Spuddled half border round Erica. Potted 6 32's Spiraeas.

Sweeping up etc

*'Native to the seacoasts of Europe and Eastern Asia, asparagus is known for its tolerance of salt. In fact, some lore has gardeners discouraging weeds by dousing asparagus beds with salt. A mixture of 1 to 2 pounds of salt (NaCl) dissolved in a gallon of water can be sprayed or sprinkled on the bed, but not on emerging spears or young ferns. This won't entirely eliminate the weeding chore, but it can help.' www.burpee.com

The diary for 1949

Mar 21st   Planted Sharpe's Express. Sowed Pansy outdoors. Spuddled round rest of Erica. Unpacked and labelled bulbs. Montbretia, Japonicas, Lilies etc.

Boxed begonias. Potted 2 doz Carnations in small 60's. Planted Montbretias, Lilies, Tigridias etc.

Planted Penstemons & Gladiolas. Mowed lawn with spinner.

Potted Carnations in 32's. Digging Shrubbery.

Top-dressed Carnations in 32's. Digging Shrubbery. Clipped Jasmine. Hoeing in K.G.

Sweeping etc.

Mar 28th   Digging in K.G. Sowed Brassicas and Leeks. Hoed through wallflowers etc. round house.

C   Digging up Daffs, Ericas & Rhodos for water pipe. Pruning roses.

O   Sowed May Queen pots, Carrots, Beet, Lettuce & Little Marvel Pea. Rose pruning.

L

D   Planted out cauliflowers and lettuce. Dug up and laid in Ericas etc. for water main. Rose pruning.

April

⚜ ⚜ ⚜

Apr 1st   Nice Day! Sowed hardy annuals in K.G. Dug up Daffs and planted in orchard. Mowed lawn rotoscythe. Sweeping up etc.

Advertised for £75 in 1952 (equivalent over £2,000 in 2020. Mr Ricks, a builder, may have purchased it at trade prices.)

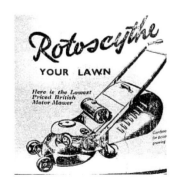

The diary for 1949

Apr 5th   Took up turf for water main. Planted 12 lilies & 100 Gladiolas. Potted 35 Mums. Sowed Cucumbers.

Split Orchid and potted into three bowls. Potted Toms in large 60's. Potted off dozen in small 60's. Sowed Ageratum, Ursinia, Zinnias, Coleus, Dahlia, Aster & Statice. Shifted plants in front of Kitchen for Water main. Rose pruning.

Sowed Cucumber Ridge & Marrows. Put out first batch of Mums in cold frame. Sowed French (cloche) Beans. Staked first Peas. Pricked out Lettuce from 1st sowing outside. Put 5 doz new Dahlias in cold frame. Rose pruning.

HAIL WIND RAIN SUN

Got out Runner Bean trench. Digging in K.G. Planted Potato – Dunbar Rover. Put rest of Dahlias in cold frame, covered peat. Rose pruning.

Mowed lawn with rotoscythe. Filled in Runner Bean trench. Replanting Erica, Polyanthus and Daffs. Sprayed with Lime Sulphur *[a spray for deciduous trees to control fungi, bacteria and insects on the bark surface]*.

Sweeping etc.

Apr 11th   Sowed Pea-Daffodil. Sowed 2nd lot annuals Zinnias, Asters, Alyssum etc. Sowed Lettuce and Carrots. Replanted Ericas, Rhodos, Daffs.

Made up Myosotis. Sowed 3 sorts Broccoli L.Q., S.N. & A.G. also cauliflower. Finished rose pruning along border, weeded and edged.

Potted another batch Mums and Cars. Pricked out Verbena. Dug and manured rose border.

Sowed Marrows. Put out one row Cauliflower & Lettuce. Mowed lawn twice with new machine.

Watering

Sweeping etc.

Son of the Secret Gardener

Apr 19th (Tues) Earthed up Potatoes. Hoeing in K.G. Top-dressed Sp Cabbage Sulph. Ammonia*. Edged up all round. Hoed and watered Polys. Hoed centre rose bed. Hosed fruit on walls.

Split up and replanted S.F. Mums in frame. Digging and hoeing in K.G. Mowing.

Pricked out nine boxes annuals. Put Begonias (F.R.) in cold house. Sowed Peas (Daisy).

Pricked out 3 boxes Dianthus. Planted out and sowed Lettuce. Split up and planted 3 doz Violets. Mowing. Went over strip with cultivator (K.G.). Pruned Forsythia, Witch Hazel, Ericas etc.

*Sulph. Ammonia - Ammonium Sulphate, was a fertiliser used for its properties of lowering the pH balance of alkaline soils and adding nitrogen to aid growth. Unclear what was used to spray fruit trees and roses on April 26th

Apr 25th Pricked out 5 boxes annuals. Potted 36 new Mums 48's, potted Toms in 48's (12) L. 60's (12) Sm. 60's (12). Planted Gladiolas. Planted Potato British Queen.

Cleared out Malacoides (Primula) (took seed) also Cinerarias. Pricked out 6 boxes Celery 1 Celeriac, 2 Ageratum & 1 Coleus. Sprayed fruit trees 7 roses 18 galls.

Pricking out more annuals. Weeded and spuddled one border.

Staked 2nd Peas. Weeded and spuddled other border. Sowed Carrots, Beet.

Mowing. Disbudding* fruit trees. Sowed Lettuce. Hoeing.

Sweeping up etc. Sowed Lettuce & Cress. Sow Obconica, Malacoides etc. Prims. [Indoor primulas]

*Disbudding: fruit trees tend to produce more fruit that the tree can support. Disbudding reduces the number of fruits, reducing the weight of fruit load and helping to prevent alternate years with little or no fruit.

May

May 2nd Top dressed first two lots peas and cauliflowers Sulph. Amm. Hoeing in KG. Potted half Begonias – 48's and 60's. Disbudding fruit trees. Hoeing in front drive.

Did cold potting. Disbudding and watering fruit trees. Put lawn sand on. Hoeing Ericas.

Spraying and disbudding wall fruit. Put naphthalene* on brassica plot and levelled. Hoeing in KG. Sowed lettuce.

Stopped S F mums. Took box cuttings. Dug over frame and prepared for box stuff. Sowed runner beans. Prepared 2 celery trenches. Edged up all round.

Mowing. Pruning

shrubs. Hoeing. Potted on doz. Cars. In L. 60's & S. 48's. Put out new mums in cold frame. Weeded & hoed Raspberries. Replanted Musk & put out Pansies. Sprayed Peaches in house.

*Naphthalene was used as a 'fumigant pesticide' and was the main active ingredient in mothballs. Products containing naphthalene have been banned in the EU since 2008 because of health risks.

May 10th [4° frost.] Sowed Savoys, Purple Sprouting, Xmas Drumhead etc Sowed Wallflowers. Planting out outdoor sown Annuals.

4° frost is more likely to mean four degrees of frost (i.e. -2° C) rather than a temperature of 4° F which would be the equivalent of minus 15° C - very unlikely, especially in May.

Sow wallflowers fortnight later [in margin]

Mowing. Sprayed fruit & roses. 24 galls. Sowed Sweet Williams.

Took cuttings of new mums. Sowed odd biennials, French Beans & Pea – Chancellor. Staked 3rd Peas.

Mowing. Potted Toms in 16's & 48's. New Cars in 48's & Toms in L. 60's.

STARTED OVERTIME

The summer was a good time to earn more money working overtime. Whether this was for his main employer or for various jobbing gardening, it was a welcome supplement to a low income.

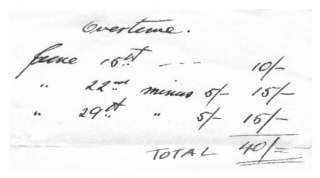

The diary for 1949

May 16th Pricked off Statice. Did odd potting. Put out S.F. Mums. Staking on border.

Sprayed Cherries. Mowing. Weeding. Put out Calceolarias in rose bed. Staking on border.

Prepared soil for Mums. Put out Brussels & Cauliflowers. Weeding.

Weeding and Hoeing. Staking herbaceous stuff.

Mowing. Weeding and Hoeing. Put out more hardy annuals. Staked 4th peas.

Weeding, Sweeping etc.

May 23rd RAIN Potted Mums in 48's. Stood out geraniums in frames. Sowed Peas – Provost.

Mowing, weeding and hoeing. Odd staking. Weeded Iris bed. Bringing out annuals.

Weeding etc. put out Broccoli. Planted Sweet Wivelsfield* in centre bed. Started clipping Deutzias.

Chelsea Show

Mowing. Edging up. Hoeing and weeding. Sweeping.

* The well-known folk musician Martin Carthy recorded an album called 'Sweet Wivelsfield' and according to notes on the website, 'There is a dianthus called "Sweet Wivelsfield" which the internationally famous carnation growers Allwood Bros named after the village in which their nurseries were, Wiveslfield Green in West Sussex.'
https://mainlynorfolk.info/martin.carthy/records/sweetwivelsfield.html

The RHS Spring Show has been held at Chelsea since 1913 with breaks during the wars. The show re-started in 1947. George's ticket would have been purchased by his employer. This would have been quite an event for him and probably his only visit, though as we have seen, he went to and exhibited at many local horticultural shows.

May 30th Sowed Cinerarias, Primulas, Calceolarias etc. Staked Runne Beans. Potted fresh stock Cars. 48's (17)

Mowing. Staked S.F. mums. Hoeing and weeding.

June

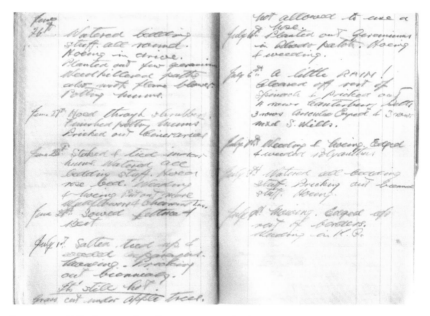

June 1st Filled up and tied Runners. Staked Tomatoes. Hoeing & Weeding. Potted Cars. 60's

Cleared off Wallflowers. Limed, dug and planted P.C. Geraniums round house.

Started mowing (RAIN). Sowed Primulas etc. 2nd batch. Finished mowing. Finished bedding round house.

June 6th Bank Holiday

Mowing. Sowed and staked Runners. Princeps. Sowed Pea – Daffodil & Lettuce. Weeded, fed & hoed carrots and beet. Filled up Cauliflowers & Brussels. Planted Helichrysum and Statice.

Bedded out Asters, Zinnias Ageratum etc in drive. Staking on border.

Planted out Dahlias. Sprayed fruit and roses 25 galls. Weeding and hoeing.

Mowing. Staked Peas Chancellor. Thinning lettuce, hoeing etc.

June 13th Planting out Dahlias and all odd bedding stuff. Filled up Caul flowers and Brussels. Hoeing and weeding.

Cut first Cauliflower and Beetroot. Preparing for potting Carnations. Mowing.

Potted 24 Cars in 48's. Planted out Purple Sprouting, Curly Kale and Cauliflower. Put out Begonias.

Planted out Celery and Celeriac. Edged up all round. Weeding.

Dig first potatoes. Mowing. Staked Provost Peas. Putting out odd bedding stuff.

June 19th Started potting mums. Odd jobs in K.G.

Watered bedding stuff all round. Put out Fuchsias in H.B. Sprayed potatoes Bordeaux mixture*. Staking on H.B.

Put out Leeks, 1 row. Put out 230 Golden ... and 130 Golden Dwarf. [Solidago?] Trimmed Aubretia on Rockery.

Put out 90 Blood Red. Potting mums, Hoeing.

Mowing. Pinched, tied and hoed S.F. Mums. Watering with Sprinkler.

Fortnight without rain.

Boiler and pipes put in new [green]house.

DIG FOR VICTORY
LEAFLET No. 9

**HOW TO MAKE
BORDEAUX**
AND
**BURGUNDY
MIXTURES**
IN
SMALL QUANTITIES

*Bordeaux mixture: copper sulphate (CuSO4) and slaked lime (Ca(OH)2), used as a fungicide, much used in vineyards, fruit-farms and gardens to prevent infestations of fungus infections including potato blight.

'…there are other chemicals that gardeners have long used with impunity, in the mistaken belief that they pose no risk to humans or wildlife. Take Burgundy mixture or Bordeaux mixture, both copper-sulphate sprays used as a preventative fungicide on potato crops and still seen by some kitchen gardeners as an entirely safe organic alternative to Dithane (now also withdrawn)… copper is a heavy metal which gradually accumulates in the soil, with unpleasant consequences for earthworms and, some studies suggest, for human health.' Fionnuala Fallon, *Irish Times* Jan 4th 2014

June 26th Watered bedding stuff all round. Hoeing in drive.
Planted out few geraniums. Weed-killered paths also with flame blower. Potting mums.

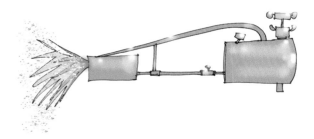

Hoed through shrubbery. Finished potting mums. Pricked our Cinerarias.

Staked and tied indoor mums. Watered all bedding stuff. Hoed rose bed. Weeding and hoeing. Put out more wallflowers & Cheiranthus.

Sowed lettuce and beet.

July

July 1st   Salted, tied up and weeded asparagus. Mowing.
         Pricking out biennials.

         It's still hot.

         Grass cut under apple trees.

         Not allowed to use a hose.

Hosepipe bans, then as now, were quite common in summer months. Only 13mm of rain fell in June and the dry weather continued until mid-July when thunder-storms started a period of unsettled weather and significant amounts of rain.

Temperatures rose to nearly 86°F (30°C) in the London area.

The diary for 1949

July 5th   Planted out Geraniums in Rhodo patch. Hoeing and weeding.

A little RAIN! Cleared off rest of Spinach & pricked out 4 rows Canterbury Bells 3 rows Auricula & 3 rows mxd S. Wills. *[Sweet Williams]*

Weeding and hoeing. Edged & weeded Polyanthus.

Watered all bedding stuff. Pricked out biennial stuff. Hoeing.

Mowing. Edged up rest of borders. Weeding in K.G.

July 11th   Picked first tomatoes. Went round K.G. Glads etc. Artificial D.B.

Watered all bedding stuff & H.B. Clearing H.B. dead blooms etc. cleared off Little Marvel & Daffodil Peas. Weeding & hoeing.

Dusted & sprayed K.G. Sowed Myosotis *[forget-me-not]* Pricked out 5 rows mixed Wallflowers. Hoed back drive. Put out 6 rows mxd Wallflowers.

Potted 6 cars 32's. Cleared up back drive. Top-dressed Cucs. Dug May Queen spuds.

Mowing. Tied in climbers. Tidying up H.B. Hoeing in K.G. Staking Dahlias.

July 16th   RAIN

Finished potting Cars 32's. pricked off more Cinerarias. Made up Canterbury Bells, Wallflowers, etc. sowed Spring Cabbage, Carrots and Lettuce.

LEFT OFF RAINING!

Sprayed Brassicas. Laying in Peaches, Plums etc.

Finished wall fruit. Hoeing. Pricked off more Cinerarias & Primulas.

Hoeing. Cleared off 1st Dwarf Beans. Bed Down Lupins & Delphs K.G.

Pruned Apple cordons. Weeding.

HOTTER THAN EVER!

The rain of the previous week was obviously not sufficient and a good deal of hand-watering was needed. Water would be stored in large galvanised tanks into which the watering cans could be dipped. These were situated by – or often inside - outbuildings and glasshouses and filled, like the more domestic barrels, from rainwater. Does 'cleared out' (below) mean cleaning the tanks or that they were emptied because so much water was needed?

July 25th   Watering H.B. Cleared out 3 garden tanks. Dusted Greenhouse*. Watered all bedding stuff.

Watering in K.G. Top dressed Dahlias, Gladiolas etc with manure. Started putting 2nd stakes to S.F. mums.

Watered and top-dressed dry Rhododendrons. Weeding and raking.

Continued S.F. mums. Weeding and watering.

Mowing. Hoed and cleared up under apples Rhodos. Edged up all round.

Sunday. RAIN!

(Start disbudding mums)

*'Dusted Greenhouse' did not mean some light housework but rather using a pesticide in powder form.

July 31st   Bank Holiday WIND & RAIN

August

❦ ❦ ❦

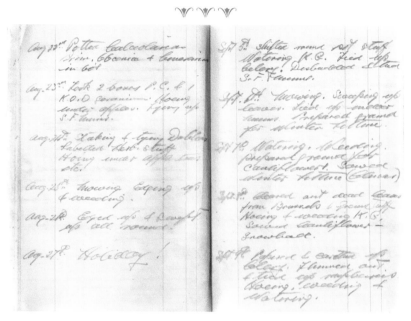

Aug 1st RAIN

Pricked out 7 rows H.S. forget-me-nots. Prepared soil & pots for Cyclamen corms. Pricked out Cins and Prims. outside.

Staking and tying up in H.B. Tied up mums. Clipping shrubs. Staking Glads & Dahlias. Tied up branches of fruit trees in orchard.

Tying up odd mums. Sooting. Clipped yew hedge outside.

Clipping yew hedge. Mowing. Dug 3rd spuds. Dunbar Rover V.G. sowed 2nd lot Spring Cabbage & Lettuce.

Horsell Grange was a substantial garden and included a small orchard. It was, however, not as large as Dorian with its tennis courts and croquet lawn. An end to rolling and maintaining tennis courts must have been a great relief!

Aug 8th Cut back laurel hedge. Clipped shrubs round house. Stood out mums. Sterilised soil for Cyclamen.

Finished clipping yew hedge. Clearing up. Cleared off rest of peas & dwarf beans.

Potted up Cyclamen, Freesias and Lachenalias.

Potted and boxed Cinerarias, Prims etc. Hoeing and weeding. Stored Beet. Cut off dead roses.

Mowing. Hoeing.

Started Greenhouse

Aug 18th Watering all round. Lifted carrots. Weeding & hoeing. Went through H.B. staking & weeding. Potting Cinerarias & Primulas.

Pruned Blackcurrants. Cleared out G.house & frames for repairs.

Diarrhoea! Sprayed mums & celery. Disbudding mums.

Mowing.

Aug 22nd Potted Calceolarias, Prim, Obconica & Cineraria in 60's.

Took 2 boxes P.C. & 1 K.O.D. geranium. Hoeing under apples. Tying up S.F. mums.

Staking and tying Dahlias. Labelled Herb. stuff. Hoeing under apple trees etc.

Mowing. Edging up & weeding.

Edged up and swept up all round.

Holiday!

The earliest holidays I can remember were taken in Clacton on the Essex coast, which, being on the other side of London, would have been very inconvenient. It is likely that Dad knew someone who let us have our caravan at a cheap rate. The caravan was in fact a Romany vehicle on a site mainly occupied by more conventional caravans. However, at this stage after the war, all sorts of vehicles had been pressed into service and I was very impressed by those who holidayed in converted buses or train carriages.

September

❦ ❦ ❦

Sept 5th   Shifted round pot stuff. Watering K.G. Tied up Celery. Disbudded & tied S.F. Mums.

Mowing. Sweeping up leaves. Tied up indoor mums. Prepared ground for Winter Lettuce.

Watering. Weeding. Prepared ground for Cauliflowers. Sowed Winter Lettuce (Clubber)

Cleared out dead leaves from Brussels & Green stuff. Hoeing & weeding K.G. Sowed Cauliflower – Snowball.

Papered & earthed up Celery. Thinned out and tied up raspberries. Hoeing, weeding & watering.

Sept 12th Watering & Hoeing.

Cleared up raspberry bed. Hoeing.

Mowing. Put out Spring Cabbage.

RAIN! Cleared out tank in G.H. Sorted out seeds.

Clearing, weeding, hoeing etc.

Sept 19th Pruning climbers by house.

Continued roses. Papered Celery.

Earthed up celery 2 rows. Housed Carnations. RAIN ALL DAY

Housed Orchids etc. Put earwig traps on Mums. Disbudding. Potted Primulas in 60's. Got flowers for Harvest Festival.

Did flowers for Harvest Festival. Mowing.

RAIN

Drying Hydrangeas & Rosemary

The Harvest Festival would probably have been at Horsell Church. In spite of our house being Horsell Lodge Cottage,

Horsell village was somewhere we visited very rarely; there was no cause to go there as the shops were in Woking town. I don't recall my parents setting foot in a church except for weddings, christenings and funerals, though they (or rather my mum) were keen on sending the children to Sunday School.

26th – 28th Holiday

29th Sept Disbudding Mums. Spraying Celery & Mums. Cutting Statice. Took 2 boxes P.C. & 1 K.O.D. Geranium cuttings. Got in Lime rubble.

Dusted Celery & green stuff Derris [a slow acting insecticide]. Picked over Celery. Mowing. Started putting in bulbs for spring.

October

Oct 1st   Dusted Celery. Made up Sp Cabbage.

Put in Lilium Candidum *[Madonna Lily]* Dug up Fuchsias & bedding Begonias. Dug up Beet sowed 29/6. Very good. Got up all odd geraniums.

Put Cyclamen in House. Potting & taking cuttings odd geraniums. Dug up Begonias, P.C. & K.O.D. Gers. Boxed Calceolarias.

Potted dozen Cinerarias. Potting P.C. Gers. Potted Coleus 48's.

Potting K.O.D. Gers. Cleared up apples. Potted crocus for forcing & Crocus Species & Hardy Cyclamen for beds to be prepared.

The diary for 1949

Cleared off border round house & put on 6 barrows manure.
Mowing. Disbudding indoor Mums etc.

Oct 10th   Dug round house. Started housing Mums.

Did odd potting. Disbudding Mums and Cars. Raked dead leaves
from Greenstuff. Tying up S.F. Mums in border & Dahlias.

Cleared up leaves from Greenstuff. Staked Brussels. Got rest of
Mums in. Tied up S.F. Mums K.G.

Potted indoor Mums from K.G.
Edged up all round. Mowing.

Sprayed Celery. Sweeping up.

Oct 17th   Pricked out Lettuce in frame.
Boxed verbenas.
Potted Ursinia (trial).
Started planting
Wallflowers round house.

THE WIND & THE RAIN!!!*

Restaked and tied up P/B... Finished planting Wallflowers (600
Cleared out tank in K.G.

Put Begonias in G House. Dipped Cinerarias. Put Freesias
Lachenalias in G house. Bedded out 200 Forgetmenots and
60 Cheiranthus.

Raked leaves from Greenstuff. Started papering Celery. Emptied
water from shelter & sorted & stored potatoes (British Queen).

Finished papering Celery. Sweeping up. Hoed & raked off leaves
from Rhodos in drive. No mowing.

*Could this be a reference to the song from *Twelfth Night*?

> When that I was and a little tiny boy,
> With a hey, ho, the wind and the rain,
> A foolish thing was but a toy,
> For the rain it raineth every day.
>
> But when I came to man's estate,
> With hey, ho, the wind and the rain,
> 'Gainst knaves and thieves men shut their gate,
> For the rain it raineth every day.
> (etc)

Oct 24th   Lit G'house fire. Sorted out bulbs and put out .....S d'Or & Iris Sustain & -?- in cold frame. Dug up Gladiolas and Tigridias.

RAIN! Dug up Polyanthus in heather border & spuddling Polyanthus border.

FLOODS! Went over G'house stuff. Staked Freesias. Made shelter for boiler of G'house.

FIRST 8° FROST Finished spuddling Poly borders. Started getting up dahlias. Wheeled out 4 barrows compost. Mowing.

4° Wheeled out 4 compost. Cleared of one row Runners. Pruned Buddleia & Laurentias.

Clearing up. Clocks put back.

The lighting of the greenhouse fire would be a significant event. It was coke fired and was kept going continuously through the winter to keep the greenhouse at a temperature above freezing. It looks like good forethought given that the first frost occurs four days later.

Oct 31st   2° Wheeled out 4 compost. Changed over Mums, late ones to lean-to. Dug up rest of Dahlias. Raked dead leaves from Greenstuff. Dug & stored Celeriac.

November

Nov 1st   [4°] Cleared off 2nd Runner Beans. Wheeled out 6 compost.

Dug up Dahlias for allotment. Cut down old Asparagus beds.

[9°] Burnt up rubbish. Hoeing heather. Cleaned and boxed Gladiolas etc for storing. Started planting Narcissus in heather. Finished it and put some in orchard.

[4°] Cleaned up bone-meal in shed. Put out 50 lettuce in C. frame. Wheeling out bonfire ashes from ......

[0°] Sweeping up all round. Made up Sp. Cabbage and hoed.

RAIN Planted Anemones in Shrubbery.

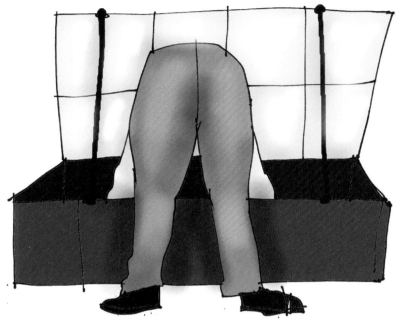

Nov 7th   Planted 2 new Rhododendrons – Handsworth Red. Going
through Cars. Etc. Dug up Rhubarb and planted half row
Malling Enterprise.

Put in rest of Raspberries – Hailshamberry*. Put C. Butt tulips in
frame. Planted A.F. [autumn flowering] Crocus Rockery.

RAIN Cut down S.F. Mums & odd herbaceous stuff in K.G.
Emptied shelter and stored Dahlias.

Fixed up shelter for ...... planted the rest of A.F. Crocus Colchcum
& Cyclamen & Ericas on Rockery.

Sweeping up all round etc.

The diary for 1949

*Hailshamberry: an extract from a Sussex History site:

My Father met my mother when he was working at Knight's Nursery in Hailsham. He drove all over East Sussex delivering fruit vegetables and garden produce. Knight's Nursery actually once invented a new fruit called the Hailshamberry!

It was first grown in 1911 and was a large, almost ever-green bush with large leaves which protected the fruit – a profusion of red berries which were a cross between a blackberry and a raspberry. According to the advertising, the new fruit 'caused a sensation' when it was exhibited at the Festival of Empire Great Fruit Show held at Crystal Palace.

They seem to have been popular until the 1940s – are they still about?' Quirky Sussex History by Kevin Gordon
https://sussexhistory.net/2016/01/09/the-hailshamberry/

Nov 14th Wheeled out 3 compost. Cut Mums for house. Mowing*.

Wheeled out 6 compost. Prepared spaces for new stock and top-dressed Asparagus beds with manure.

Dug up Solidago on border. Started clearing same.

Dug up S.F. Mums & put in cold frame.

FOG Sweeping leaves.

*Surely the last mowing of the season?

Nov 21st Pricked out 3 pans Winter Lettuce. Started Rose pruning.

Rose pruning.

Rose pruning.

Sowed Cress and mustard. Put some Cinerarias in cold house. Pricked out 2 boxes pansies. Planted crocus and forgetmenots in vases. Cutting down more stuff on H. border.

Sweeping up all round.

Nov 28th   Raked up Br. Sprout leaves.
            Started tying in Roses.

            Sweeping in drive. Cont. tying in Roses. Went through
            frames. Rose tying in.

One can get some idea of the size of rose beds from the fact that the
best part of three days was spent pruning and the following week a
similar amount of time tying them in.

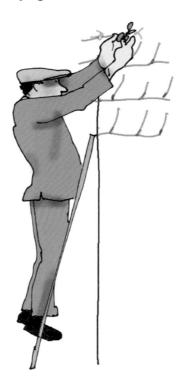

November

Dec 1st   Finished Roses. Burnt rubbish. Got flowers and plants for
bazaar*. Put Begonias in shelter. Sweeping & clearing up.

***A Christmas Bazaar presumably. As with the Harvest Festival, the
owners of large gardens would want to demonstrate their largesse.**

Dec 5th   Dipped Primulas and Calceolarias.

          Cutting down and thinning out on Herbaceous Border.

          Ditto. Wheeled on manure.

          Started digging on border.

          Continued digging on H.B.

          Dragged lawn. Sweeping up all round.

Dec 12th   Pruned Wisteria and Pyrocanthus on H.B. New Roses came
            H.T. shifted Cinerarias and Mums from cold house.

            Digging on H.B.

            Digging on H.B.

            Finished digging on H.B. Raked up Brussel leaves.

            Planted Iris in shrubbery. Sweeping up all round.

Dec 19th   Sowed Mustard Cress. Topped 4 apple and 1 pear tree.
            To be pulled out.

            Started pruning. Put in boxes Mustard Cress &
            Lettuce – May King.

            Put in 4 pots Celeriac for forcing. Wheeling in soil in
            frame. Pruning.

            Finished Pruning Apples. Dragged lawn. Sweeping up all round.

The diary for 1949

Christmas Day was on the Saturday, so holidays got moved to the following Monday and Tuesday. In addition, it seems Dad had Friday off; five days for Christmas – a luxury. Christmases were a happy time for me, except for the one year when my parents had flu. It may not have been unalloyed pleasure for my mum, especially when grandparents visited. My father's father was not easy to get on with. My mum's parents were easier, though they could be a strain as they came from London and stayed with us. Where everyone slept, I can't work out. Probably grandparents had my parents' room and my parents slept downstairs somehow.

Dec 28th Started pruning wall fruit. Raked up leaves in Chicken Run. Coke for boiler.

Started enlarging bed on lawn for Roses. Got up collection H.P. for Mr. W. Got up carrots. Light for boiler.

Started on centre bed. Got out Almond & Holly trees. Shifted Peonies. Continued pruning wall fruit.

Epilogue

Dad was a gentle man, though stubborn at times, and while he was not one to share emotions, he was a wonderful father. We were always playing games, indoors and out. Our modest lawn became a tennis or badminton court (no lines of course), a croquet lawn (proper iron hoops acquired from who knows where), or a putting green. My friends loved to visit and perhaps play billiards in the kitchen where there was hardly room to swing a cue.

Our council house had a good-sized garden and he planted apple trees, currants, raspberries and gooseberries, all of which thrived. I don't recall vegetables as clearly but there were definitely runner beans and cabbages. He and I, with help from my brother-in-law, John, built a greenhouse from wood and polythene at the bottom of the garden. This survived a couple of paraffin stove incidents, one of which left his cactus collection with a permanent sooty tidemark. Eventually it was replaced with something more permanent. Health and safety were not high in Dad's priorities.

I realise my mum has not featured much in this book, partly because it is after all, about Dad, but also because she left almost no documents apart from photographs and her certificate of completion of apprenticeship. Nevertheless, she was the person around whom the life of the house centred. She was delighted to move to our council house and loved to make small improvements – a piece of furniture, some wallpapering, an ornament... She was also a formidable manager of money given the poor wages Dad received; he never earned enough to pay income tax, for example.

She survived my dad by several decades, living well into her nineties. She kept the garden going as best she could, with the help of family and neighbours. I should also mention that after Dad died, she received some very welcome support from the Gardeners' Benevolent Society (now 'Perennial'). Should this book ever return a profit, those monies will be donated to them.

My Father's Hands

The hands that tuck the tuber gently into bed
that lift his son onto his shoulders
are the same that break the shiny slugs in half,
that snap them like black sausages
and throw them to the birds in bits.
He keeps his fingernails long and strong
precisely for this work; returns each day
with crescents of deep black, the richest soil.
Each mealtime's grace a ritual scraping out
of nails with clasp knife, honed and worn with work.
In winter, these same hands wear leather gloves
mended time and time again – and sewn
and patched with twine: make do and mend.
He feels, like seeds and corms and tubers,
these too, once buried in the garden shed,
left long enough, might then be new again.

About the Author

Although he is the grandson of the Secret Gardener, Trevor Millum ended the long line of gardeners and became a teacher and, along the way, a writer. Books and resources for teachers have been a constant, reflecting a varied 'career' as advisor, software manager, Director of NATE and writer-in-schools. He has published short stories for adults and young readers but is best known as a children's poet, featuring in over 200 anthologies together with collections such as *Warning, Too Much Schooling Can Damage Your Health* and *A Stegosaurus is For Life*. It seems a long way from his first publication, Images of Woman – *Advertising in Women's Magazines*... He lives in Barrow-upon-Humber where he has his own (almost) secret garden.

Twink Addison was born and brought up in a small village on the Lincolnshire Marsh, where she lives today. She is a gardener and cartoonist.

Acknowledgement

Thanks to Dan Pearson, who helped me with some of the tricky plant abbreviations. His *Natural Selection – a year in the garden* has also been an inspiration.